Elopers' Wedding Song

Today we walk, side by side,
Down the aisle of our love;
No trumpets blare, no church bells ring,
There is no veil or satin glove.

Today we join our hearts together,
Beneath the setting sun;
With God our only invited guest,
As our lives merge into one.

There are no Scriptures, no Bible here,
To tell us how to wed;
Instead we have God's gentle ocean,
His soft, white sand, and His flower bed.

We pledge our promise to love fore'er
Then we walk along the quiet beach;
No rice is thrown, no limo waits,
There's no First Dance or Best Man's Speech.

We watch the sunlight fade away,
As we gaze at the golden rings on our hands,
And we delight in our perfect wedding day,
Without its pomp and circumstance.

Your Unique Wedding

SAY "I DO" WITH A TWIST!

Kerry McDonald

A division of The Career Press, Inc.
Franklin Lakes NJ

YOUR UNIQUE WEDDING
EDITED AND TYPESET BY KATE HENCHES
Cover design by DesignConcept
Printed in the U.S.A. by Book-mart Press

To order this title, please call toll-free 1-800-CAREER-1 (NJ and Canada: 201-848-0310) to order using VISA or MasterCard, or for further information on books from Career Press.

The Career Press, Inc., 3 Tice Road, PO Box 687,
Franklin Lakes, NJ 07417

www.careerpress.com
www.newpagebooks.com

Library of Congress Cataloging-in-Publication Data

McDonald, Kerry A.
    Your unique wedding : say "I do" with a twist / Kerry A. McDonald.
        p. cm.
    Includes index.
    ISBN 1-56414-751-7
    1. Weddings. 2. Weddings—Planning. I. Title.

HO745.M394 2005
    395.2'--dc22   2004059245

Dedication

To my husband, Brian Roughan,
who each day upholds his wedding vow
to encourage my own fulfillment as an individual.

Contents

Introduction

Soon after my husband, Brian, and I got engaged in the fall of 2000, we began to make plans for our wedding—a traditional one of course, for we didn't think there was another option. It was to be a moderate-sized wedding of about 125 people at a seaside resort. As most of today's engaged couples do, we planned for a wedding 18 months in advance, so there was plenty of time to work out details. Plans were going along well, as I booked the reception site and the church and submitted deposits. The date was set for a much-coveted Saturday in mid-June.

As the first few months of wedding planning passed, I glimpsed the chaos involved with planning a traditional wedding. Somehow I became convinced that it was perfectly acceptable to pay over $5,000 for a photographer and more than twice that for a reception dinner. But one day, as I filled out a formal wedding questionnaire from a church I had never attended for a minister I had never met, I awoke from the traditional wedding spell, put down my pen mid-sentence, and concluded that this just wasn't right for me.

The next day, as Brian jumped for joy that I had finally come to my senses, I called the Marriott Resort in Kauai, Hawaii, and within minutes had an elopement wedding date set six months in advance.

That July morning on Kalapaki Beach, Brian and I shared one of the most special moments of our lives together. Rather than marching to the pomp and circumstance that orchestrates a traditional wedding, after we said I do, we walked barefoot along the sandy beach and spent the afternoon hiking to a majestic tropical canyon.

Writing Your Unique Wedding Story

I decided to say I do with a twist. Now it is time for you to create your own unique wedding story. Although we couldn't be happier with our decision to elope to a tropical paradise, that model may not fit your specific needs and wedding-day expectations. You need to plan a wedding that's right for you. By choosing to read this book, it is clear that you are contemplating something a bit different for your wedding and are wondering which non-traditional option might be appropriate. The best thing you can do to decide whether a non-traditional wedding is right for you is to keep doing what you're doing—collect as much information as possible and think the idea through. With the panoply of traditional wedding books, planners, and bridal magazines assailing you at every newsstand and supermarket check out, you are likely to have some doubts about choosing a non-traditional wedding. This book was written to be a resource for readers who are considering a unique wedding day and are seeking non-traditional wedding ideas not found in conventional wedding literature.

While researching this book, I ran a search for books at *Amazon.com* using the keywords "non-traditional wedding." My search revealed one book. One book! Next I ran a search using the keywords "traditional wedding." That search uncovered more than 500 books. Clearly, the stewards of the $50-billion-a-year wedding industry want you to believe that no option but the traditional wedding can be meaningful and special and filled with love and sacrament. Well, they are wrong. A non-traditional wedding is absolutely something you should consider!

Your Unique Wedding will help you to answer the questions, manage the details, and address the challenges of planning a creative wedding day experience. Regardless of which wedding day path you ultimately choose, your wedding day is sure to be filled with joy and fond memories. Best wishes as you undertake this exciting life adventure!

Part I:
Exploring a
Non-Traditional
Wedding

Chapter 1

What Is a Non-Traditional Wedding?

A non-traditional wedding is anything you want it to be! When you choose a non-traditional wedding, you choose a wedding that is as unique as you are. There are no rules or precedents to follow. There are no customs to consider or obligations to obey. You create the prototype for your wedding and decide which traditions, if any, to include. For centuries, couples have thought that they have only two options when getting married: plan a traditional wedding or elope. Today, couples are realizing that there are many other choices within the non-traditional wedding spectrum.

A non-traditional wedding is an extraordinary celebration that does not follow the etiquette standards and matrimonial requirements characteristic of conventional nuptials. Perhaps you choose an exciting wedding venue, fly away to a far-off destination, get married on Halloween, or surprise your wedding day guests. Your non-traditional wedding is unlike any other that your guests would likely encounter. It is designed with a creative spirit and perfected with close collaboration by you and your partner. It is generally less expensive than a traditional wedding and allows much more flexibility with invitations, food, locations, decorations, and attire. It can be elegant, outrageous, or something in between.

It can be religious, secular, or a combination of the two. It is fun for you and your loved ones and will keep people talking for years to come. A non-traditional wedding is many things, but most importantly it is a special occasion for you and your partner to showcase your ingenuity and devotion.

This book highlights five types of non-traditional weddings and offers planning tips for these weddings and other unique wedding alternatives. You will learn how to plan a private elopement; invite your family and friends to a destination wedding; surprise your guests on your wedding day; select and prepare for a theme wedding; and consider an adventure wedding by land, sea, or air. If you already know the type of wedding you want to plan, then feel free to skip ahead to the appropriate chapter. If you are exploring non-traditional wedding options, then you will find the checklists, planning tips, and personal and inpirational stories of other unique weddings to be helpful. You may decide to plan a non-traditional wedding unlike any described in this book. Go for it! The strategies presented here will prepare you for whichever unique wedding you choose.

Evolution of Traditional Weddings

As you endeavor to decide if a non-traditional wedding is right for you, it may be worth thinking about the evolution of the traditional wedding as the primary choice for today's couples. Traditional weddings have their roots in religious and social mores. Until the 20th century, weddings were an occasion to pass property (namely a bride and her dowry) from the bride's family to the groom. The traditional customs of "giving the bride away" and showering new couples with gifts are remnants of these earlier matrimonial norms.

Where Do Wedding Traditions Come From?

Most modern wedding traditions originate from ancient and medieval times, when fertility, virginity, luck, and avoiding evil spirits were top priorities for marrying couples.

> **Best Man.** This was the strongest man a groom would ask to accompany him when kidnapping a bride in medieval times.

> **Bouquet Toss.** Luck would be passed from a married woman to her husbandless friends when the bride tossed her flowers.

> **Bridal Party.** Bridesmaids and ushers were used to confuse evil spirits who, it was thought, would try to interfere with a couple's luck. With women dressed like the bride and men dressed like the groom, the evil spirits would not know who the lucky couple was.

> **Bride on the Left.** The groom needed his right hand free to quickly reach for his sword.

> **Flowers.** Fertility.

> **Giving the Bride Away.** Property passed from a bride's family to a groom.

> **Honeymoon.** This was the month-long hiding period following a bridal kidnap when the groom would feed his bride a concoction of honey and mead to keep her intoxicated.

> **Receiving Line.** The bride and groom were thought to be blessed and anyone who touched them would receive good luck.

> **Throwing rice.** Blessing of fertility and abundance.

> **Veil.** Youth and virginity.

As women gained independence from their families and husbands in the latter half of the 20th century, acceptance of non-traditional weddings increased; yet, spending on large, traditional weddings surged. Intimate weddings in a family's parlor that were characteristic of the early 1900s were replaced with large and expensive traditional weddings in the second half of the century.

Why would couples with new-found social independence living in a more tolerant society choose lavish traditional weddings? The answer: Mr. and Mrs. Jones. The Baby Boomers were expected to keep up with their neighbors and demonstrate to their social circles that they could purchase the same big wedding as everyone else. Today, keeping up with the Joneses is not enough. We need to surpass them. Consumer trends of the past two decades show that people are increasingly purchasing more than they can afford and are spending their income on luxuries more than necessities.[1] These luxuries include big, traditional weddings that middle-class families purchase even though it often thrusts them into debt. In fact, many couples and their families take years to pay off wedding purchases charged to their credit cards, and for some couples the burden of wedding debt brought into the marriage is a catalyst for divorce.[2]

The Rise of Traditional Wedding Alternatives

Wedding-related expenses, which consume approximately 12.5 percent of all retail dollars spent in the United States each year, are skyrocketing to an average wedding price-tag of more than $22,000, excluding the honeymoon. And that is for an *average* wedding. Many people will easily spend two or three times that for a deluxe wedding day. For example, couples marrying in New York City will spend an average of $33,424 on their weddings.[3]

This is a significant amount of money—money that some engaged couples decide would be better spent paying off college loans, placing a down payment on a nice home, or investing in a retirement plan. With nearly 60 percent of today's couples paying for some or all of their wedding expenses, it is no wonder that couples are looking for alternatives to the costs and constraints associated with a traditional wedding.[4] Today hundreds of thousands of couples choose to plan something different for their wedding celebrations. For example, 8 percent of the 2.3 million weddings performed each year are estimated to be destination weddings, or "weddingmoons," where the bride and groom, and often a few close loved ones, travel to distant places to celebrate a wedding away.

In addition to the nearly 200,000 weddingmooners, many couples are choosing surprise weddings, last-minute getaway weddings, outdoor adventure weddings with friends and family, and theme weddings to add animation to a wedding celebration and allow the guests to become more involved. As ethnic, cultural, and religious integration grows, multicultural couples are seeking ideas on how to create new traditions on their wedding days. Many more couples are considering ways to retain the characteristics of a traditional wedding, but add some inventive, non-traditional components to their special day. Of course, the prototypical elopement on the steps of city hall remains alive and well. On a busy day at San Francisco's city hall, for instance, city officials marry six couples per hour.[5] And in 2003 the first wedding-in-space ceremony was performed aboard the International Space Station!

As you will see in this book, the army of couples who embrace wedding alternatives is steadfast and growing. Even in the length of time it took to write this book, more and more articles and Websites emerged to offer information and support to think-different couples. Vital statistics also point to an increase in the number of non-traditional weddings. Marriage data from two of the country's most popular wedding destinations, Hawaii and Las Vegas, have reported steady marriage increases over the past several years. In Hawaii, 18,118 people married in 1994, compared to 22,873 in 1999. The breakdown of these numbers shows that the percentage of non-Hawaiian residents getting married in the state has steadily surpassed residents during the past few years, indicating far more people choosing a destination wedding to Hawaii. In 1994, 48.6 percent of marriages performed in Hawaii were ones in which neither bride nor groom was a Hawaiian resident, and by 1997 that number increased to 55.5percent.[6] We see similar marriage trends in Clark County, Nevada (home to Las Vegas), where nearly 116,000 marriages were conducted in 1999, and more than 123,000 marriages were conducted in 2001.[7] *Time* Magazine reported, in May 2003, that wedding planners in two other popular weddingmoon destinations, the Caribbean and Florida, saw destination wedding rates surge from 40 percent to 80 percent in just two years![8]

In the mid-1950s, when the idea of a non-traditional wedding was anathema, the average age of first marriage was roughly 22.5 for men and 20 for women. According to the U.S. Census Bureau, those numbers have increased dramatically over the past half-century to a current average marrying age of approximately 27.7 for men and 25 for women. Delayed marriage among 20-somethings is largely attributed to greater investments in education and careers, and a growing acceptance of premarital sex and cohabitation. When the time finally comes for men and women to marry, there are many factors to consider. Often, these couples would prefer to invest in their homes, in their children's educations, and in their 401(k) plans.

Unlike in past years, when a non-traditional wedding meant either that the bride was pregnant or that the couple was rebelling against a disapproving family, today's non-traditional weddings are much more calculated, creative, diverse, and well-received. Today's consumer-savvy couples are marrying at more mature ages, are more highly educated, more affluent, and more independent than their parents' generations. They recognize that the traditional wedding can stifle creativity, induce stress and frustration, and fail to capture the character and romance of the marrying couple. In growing numbers, these couples are turning away from traditional weddings in favor of an individualized, innovative wedding experience.

But why might the image of a traditional wedding still be set in your mind? Why does it seem so hard to break from the prototype of a traditional wedding and plan your unique wedding?

Confronting the Traditional Wedding Monopoly

Before you can truly decide if a non-traditional wedding is right for you, you should first confront the ubiquitous influences of the "Traditional Wedding Monopoly," or the TWM. The dictionary definition of a monopoly is "exclusive possession or control; a commodity controlled by one party." The TWM, like any monopoly, seeks exclusivity by suffocating competitive information, maintaining high prices for low-quality products, taking advantage of unwitting consumers, and allocating scarce resources inefficiently—namely your precious dollars!

Over the past half-century, this $50-billion-a-year industry has stealthily invaded the psyche of every prospective bride and groom, and their loved ones, persuading us that there is no marriage alternative to the traditional wedding. Immediately upon announcing your engagement, you find yourself bombarded by traditional wedding images from pricey bridal magazines, reality television shows, and the endless talk of friends and family who sweep you into the throes of traditional wedding planning. It takes a strong will, a discerning eye, and a sense that things could be different to recognize and rebel against the TWM.

For many couples, this skepticism begins to emerge in the early stages of wedding planning. A bride, who asserts adamantly that this is *her* wedding day, soon realizes that she is not in control of her celebration. Parents who insist on a lengthy church service, a sister who refuses to wear the shoes you have selected for your bridesmaids, a best man who is opposed to wearing a tuxedo, all join forces to seize your special day. You try to fight. You continue to state that this is *your* day and demand acquiescence from your friends and loved ones, but you realize that everyone is consumed by the TWM. They insist on telling you the proper way to plan *your* day. The reality is that a traditional wedding is not yours. You are constrained by financial contributions, family perceptions, and strong emotions that wear you down. Most brides succumb to these pressures imposed by a colossal wedding industry and the loved ones who embrace it. But if you are determined to remain in control of your wedding day, then explore a wedding that isn't tied to tradition.

Once you begin to question the Traditional Wedding Monopoly and quietly start to investigate other possibilities, you discover that the traditional wedding carries an exorbitant price tag for a low-quality, undifferentiated product. Certainly you will recall traditional weddings you attended that were meaningful, but were they really worth over $22,000? After all, the monopolistic characteristics of the traditional wedding lead to a product that is essentially the same each time it is purchased.

With few exceptions, the traditional wedding product typically consists of a bride walking down a red-carpeted aisle dressed in an expensive white gown (worn only on this day), preceded by several bridesmaids dressed in equally costly and non-utilitarian—though more fluorescent—gowns. At the end of the aisle waits the groom, dressed in an expensive and undistinguishable tuxedo and surrounded by groomsmen dressed the same. Each bridesmaid and groomsman also possesses a bouquet or boutonniere, symbolizing just the tip of the extraordinarily priced flower arrangement iceberg.

Once the processional concludes, the officiant reads a few predictable passages, followed by more predictable recitations by the bride and groom. After an endless and stuffy ceremony, which most guests pray will quickly end so that they can proceed to the cocktail hour, the bride and groom frolic down the church aisle, into the traditional receiving line, into the traditional white limousine, and off to the traditional wedding reception to continue with their traditional wedding day.

At the traditional reception, the guests are herded to their tables to witness—"for the first time as husband and wife"—Mr. and Mrs. Traditional Wedding, who then do a traditional wedding day dance. A delicious dinner of rubber chicken and cold potatoes is served, followed by the traditional cake-cutting ceremony. And what traditional wedding day would be complete without the traditional bouquet toss, followed by several middle-aged women dancing the Macarena? All this for the bargain-basement price of several thousand dollars.

Well, there you have it. After four hours and a home equity loan, the traditional wedding is finally over. Some of you may be saying to yourself that this off-the-shelf product is exactly what you are looking for and definitely worth every penny. Great! You will find many resources to help you to plan your traditional wedding. But many of you are becoming increasingly certain that this cookie-cutter wedding is an inefficient use of your limited dollars. Many of you realize that the traditional wedding industry is a powerful, over-priced monopoly and you are looking to the competition for some alternatives. Now is the time for the multi-billion-dollar traditional wedding industry to experience some much-needed market competition from wary consumers like you who long to be in control of your unique wedding.

Chapter Notes

1. Juliet B. Schor, *The Overspent American. Why We Want What We Don't Need* (Perennial, 1999).

2. Jennifer Bayot, "For Richer or Poorer: To Our Visa Card Limit." *The New York Times* (13 July 2003: 1).

3. Leslie Haggin Geary, "Love is priceless." *CNN/ Money*, 02 June 2003. http://money.cnn.com/2003/05/30/ pf/saving/weddings_costs/index.htm

4. Jennifer Bayot, "For Richer or Poorer: To Our Visa Card Limit." *The New York Times* , 13 July 2003,1.

5. Carolyn Jones, "Members of the Wedding: Volunteers Turn City Hall Ceremonies into Momentous Occasions." *The San Francisco Chronicle*, 2 September 2000.

6. Hawaii State Department of Health, *Statistical Report* (annual). http://www.state.hi.us/health/stats/vs.

7. http://www.co.clark.nv.us/clerk/Annual_Stats.htm.

8. Pamela Paul, "Going Off To Get Married: The Big Day Becomes A Real Holiday When Couples Hold Their Ceremonies in Faraway Places." *Time* Magazine, 7 May 2003.

Chapter 2

Is a Non-Traditional Wedding Right for You?

While you may be frustrated by the high costs and requirements of a traditional wedding, and increasingly skeptical of the Traditional Wedding Monopoly, you may not yet be certain that a non-traditional wedding is right for you. They aren't for everyone. If you believe that your wedding day is the most important day of your life and you have been yearning since childhood for the moment to hear Pachabel's Cannon blare as you walk to the altar, then you should consider a traditional wedding. But if you think a non-traditional wedding sounds intriguing and you want some help to determine if it is right for you, try taking the Unique Wedding Self-Assessment.

Unique Wedding Self-Assessment

5=Very much so   3=Somewhat   1=Not at all

4=For the most part etc.   2=Only slightly

Directions: For each of the following statements, circle the number that is most true for you. Once you have completed the self-assessment, add up your score and analyze your results.

Note: Use a pencil, as you may want to have your part-ner try this quiz too!

Scoring

Count the number of cirles per column:

	5	4	3	2	1
1. I am a non-conformist.	5	4	3	2	1
2. I am open to new ideas.	5	4	3	2	1
3. I have many interests and hobbies.	5	4	3	2	1
4. I avoid being the center of attention.	5	4	3	2	1
5. I plan to pay for my wedding expenses.	5	4	3	2	1
6. I have financial goals that I am trying to meet (for example, buy a house, pay off loans, and so on).	5	4	3	2	1
7. I am adventurous.	5	4	3	2	1
8. I am confident when defending my decisions and actions.	5	4	3	2	1
9. I have some debt (for example, student loans, car loans).	5	4	3	2	1
10. I am financially conservative.	5	4	3	2	1
11. I make decisions based on facts and practical considerations.	5	4	3	2	1
12. I am accepting of different religious and cultural ideas.	5	4	3	2	1
13. My family and friends are sup-portive and understanding.	5	4	3	2	1
14. I frequently choose to take the road less traveled.	5	4	3	2	1
15. My partner and I have discussed a non-traditional wedding.	5	4	3	2	1

16. My wedding day is *not* the most important day of my life.   5   4   3   2   1

17. I can accept criticism.   5   4   3   2   1

18. My partner and I share many of the same interests.   5   4   3   2   1

19. I have avoided tradition in the past.   5   4   3   2   1

20. I am successful.   5   4   3   2   1

21. I don't dwell on what other people think.   5   4   3   2   1

22. I find that most weddings I've attended are very similar.   5   4   3   2   1

23. I have many professional goals and personal ambitions.   5   4   3   2   1

24. I can manage conflict and confrontation.   5   4   3   2   1

25. I am a creative thinker.   5   4   3   2   1

26. I enjoy being different from my friends.   5   4   3   2   1

27. I am a risk-taker.   5   4   3   2   1

28. I believe that my wedding day is primarily for my partner and me.   5   4   3   2   1

29. I am prepared to accept fewer wedding gifts.   5   4   3   2   1

30. My partner and I want to plan our wedding together.   5   4   3   2   1

31. My partner and I want to be in total control of our wedding experience.   5   4   3   2   1

32. I feel confident in asserting my wishes to wedding vendors.   5   4   3   2   1

33. I would like to get married within the next year.   5   4   3   2   1

34. I have a busy schedule.   5   4   3   2   1

35. My partner and I are equals.   5   4   3   2   1

36. I am a smart consumer.   5   4   3   2   1

37. My partner and I share the same values.   5   4   3   2   1

38. My partner and I frequently compromise when making decisions.   5   4   3   2   1

39. I am independent.   5   4   3   2   1

40. I feel in control of my destiny.   5   4   3   2   1

41. My partner and I fear losing control of our wedding experience.   5   4   3   2   1

42. I can think of many alternative ways to spend wedding day dollars.   5   4   3   2   1

43. I am looking to plan a frugal wedding.   5   4   3   2   1

44. I know other people who have planned non-traditional weddings.   5   4   3   2   1

45. I enjoy spending lots of time with my partner.   5   4   3   2   1

46. I like to take on new challenges.   5   4   3   2   1

47. My religious faith allows me to be flexible with traditions.   5   4   3   2   1

48. I want to avoid wedding stress.   5   4   3   2   1

49. I don't like being told what to do.   5   4   3   2   1

50. I communicate openly with my partner.   5   4   3   2   1

Number of circles per column:					
Multiply total by:	x5	x4	x3	x2	x1
List column totals:					
Add the 5 totals and your final score is:	+	+	+	+	

Self-Assessment Analysis

Definite Yes (210-250)

Skip ahead to Part II because a non-traditional wedding is exactly what you are looking for! You are an independent spirit who is not afraid to challenge cultural norms in pursuit of your own happiness and adventure. You are confident in your decisions and are able to clearly assert your wishes and expectations. You can meet criticism and confrontation head-on because you have a strong character and an open relationship with your partner. You and your partner share many interests and values and both of you want to be in control of your wedding day. You have many goals and aspirations and make practical decisions, but you like to have fun. All you need to do is to select your favorite unique wedding option and start planning!

Probably Yes (170-209)

A non-traditional wedding is probably right for you, but you may have some challenges to overcome. You are independent minded, like to have fun, and have a strong relationship with your partner based on open communication and mutual respect. You may be concerned about the reactions of family members and friends to your unique wedding and don't want to disappoint your loved ones. There may also be aspects of a traditional wedding that you do not want to ignore. Perhaps a religious ceremony witnessed by many guests is important to you. Or maybe you want your family and friends to be closely involved with your wedding planning. These hesitations should not dissuade you from planning your unique wedding. In fact, they should be helpful in steering you toward a wedding day that's right for you. You might, for example, have a formal wedding ceremony but choose a theme wedding reception. Or perhaps you and your partner could plan a private elopement and later host a big celebration party with family and friends.

Consider the elements of your wedding that are most important and plan a unique wedding day that blends creativity and convention.

Maybe (100-169)

You are on the fence about choosing a non-traditional wedding. There are many aspects of a unique wedding that appeal
to you, such as imagination and independence, but there are
certain things that are holding you back. You may have always
dreamed of being the center of attention on your wedding. You
may have loved ones who would be devastated if you choose an
unconventional wedding day. You may have strong religious
beliefs that influence your decision-making. You may also have
a lot of time and money to devote to planning a wedding. A
non-traditional wedding is certainly not out of the question for
you, but you and your partner need to seriously consider three
questions before deciding which wedding path to take:

1. What is the primary purpose of your wedding day?

Think about the driving force for your wedding day. Maybe
your wedding day is primarily about religious sacrament. Maybe
it is about pleasing others. Maybe it is about a group celebration
or a personal union. Deciding what your wedding day is meant
to do will help you to choose the style of wedding that is right
for you.

**2. What do you give up if you choose a non-traditional
wedding?**

Make a list of what you might sacrifice if you choose a unique
wedding. Then decide if there are ways to include traditional
elements within a non-traditional celebration. Often what we
think we might sacrifice can be salvaged with some creativity
and careful planning.

3. Why are you choosing a unique wedding?

If the criticism and disappointment of loved ones are keeping you from choosing a non-traditional wedding, take some
time as a couple to formulate a solid defense. By anticipating

criticism and conflict, and preparing a well-thought-out argument for why you are choosing a unique wedding, you will be better equipped to assert your wishes and plan the wedding you want.

Probably Not (50-99)

Regrettably a non-traditional wedding is probably not right for you. You may be excited about the originality and freedom of a non-traditional wedding, but there may be too many obstacles preventing you from moving ahead with a non-traditional wedding. You should feel good about your decision, though, because you are *choosing* a traditional wedding rather than letting it choose you!

Still not convinced that you should plan a unique wedding? Let's dig deeper into the 10 self-assessment statements that are most crucial to consider when choosing a non-traditional wedding.

1. Are you a busy person?

Traditional wedding planning can take a lot out of you. The average traditional wedding couple can spend up to 250 hours planning a wedding! If you are like most people in today's fast-paced, high-pressure world, you don't have 250 hours to devote to planning a four-hour party.

At some point, every bride and groom immersed in traditional wedding planning asks themselves if it's really worth all the time, aggravation, and cost. Is it really worth trying to make sure every detail is attended to and every family member is satisfied? Is it really worth forcing your bridesmaids to purchase frilly, eggplant-colored dresses for $200 a pop just so they match the lilac flowers in the church? Is it really worth arguing with your mother over which place-card holders to buy and where to seat Aunt Edna? Is it really worth listening to the nagging complaints of your future mother-in-law who insists on going all out on the wedding favors for your guests? Is it really worth feeling that your wedding is more about pleasing others than it is about pleasing yourself and your spouse-to-be?

You work hard enough during the week. You certainly don't need to take on the new full-time job of planning your wedding. Celebrating the union of two people who love each other should not be work—it should be fun! And fun is something that also often gets lost among the dyed shoes, candelabras, aisle runners, and pomp and circumstance of the traditional wedding day. If you are a busy person with a full life and many interests, then a non-traditional wedding may be for you.

2. Do you want to plan your wedding as a couple?

When you choose a non-traditional wedding, you regain control over your wedding experience and, more importantly, over the relationship that you and your partner share. Much more than in traditional weddings, when you choose a non-traditional wedding, you and your partner spend a lot of time planning your wedding together. You will find that you will collaborate on every detail from the type of flowers you may decide to purchase to the brand of champagne with which you may decide to toast your marriage. The whole idea of your wedding recaptures joy, excitement, and love. The 250 hours that you would have spent planning your traditional wedding can now be dedicated to preparing for your marriage.

3. Are you a creative thinker?

Everyone who undertakes the arduous process of planning a traditional wedding has surely toyed with the idea that a non-traditional wedding would be much easier. For many people, this is just a fleeting thought, amidst making phone calls to photographers and signing catering contracts. We are so conditioned to think that the traditional wedding is the only way for two people to get married that it is often difficult to believe that there really are wonderful wedding alternatives for couples to consider.

The truth is that while many people dream wistfully of a unique, non-traditional wedding, most couples still choose the traditional wedding route. The chance to be different, then, is enticing! It takes a bit of a non-conformist—someone who chooses to be his own person and not follow the crowd, someone who rejects the multi-billion-dollar wedding industry propaganda—to truly conceptualize and plan a non-traditional wedding.

One of the great joys of planning a non-traditional wedding is the opportunity to trade ritual for creativity, customs for originality. Planning a non-traditional wedding is entirely your own doing. There are no precedents to follow, no norms to obey, no gaffes to avoid. If you decide it is important for you to cut a cake or do a dance, then do it! Unless you decide to tie the knot on top of Mount Everest, it shouldn't be too difficult for you to incorporate any meaningful activities into your wedding day.

4. Do you have family and friends who are supportive and understanding?

You are undertaking a deliberate effort to determine whether or not a non-traditional wedding makes sense for you, but your family and friends may not have had time to conduct their own calculated assessment of the benefits of a unique wedding. Your loved ones may be caught entirely off-guard by your decision.

Many mothers, siblings, best friends, grandmothers, and neighbors have dreams of helping you to plan and execute the perfect traditional wedding. When they learn that you are choosing a non-traditional wedding, they may react in startling ways. Before you choose a non-traditional wedding, make certain that you are strong enough to accept criticism and condemnation from loved ones, and that you have enough supportive people in your life to help you through the process.

The good news is that disappointment from family and friends usually doesn't last too long. The people closest to you ultimately want you to be happy. After putting their own feelings behind them, your loved ones will likely accept the idea of a non-traditional wedding and may even begin to embrace the fun, excitement, and romance of an original wedding day adventure. Some of your friends and family may even pleasantly surprise you. For example, one bride reported that when she informed her parents of her decision to elope rather than plan a traditional wedding, her mother burst out: "Oh, that's something your father and I would have loved to do!" If you have supportive family members and friends, and are certain that you can handle their initial criticisms, then go ahead and continue with your unique wedding planning.

5. Are you prepared for fewer wedding gifts?

As selfish as it may sound, one downside of choosing a non-traditional wedding is that you may not receive as many gifts and as much attention as you would with a traditional wedding. Gifts are expected at showers, bachelor and bachelorette parties, bridal breakfasts, and, of course, on the actual wedding day. It's not unusual for wedding guests to spend more than $200 on gifts for the bride and groom. In fact, some non-traditional couples report that they spent more to attend their friends' weddings than they did on their own!

If you have a strong *quid pro quo* attitude, where you believe that you bought expensive gifts for your friends when they married and therefore they should do the same for you, then a non-traditional wedding may not be right for you. But if you believe strongly that a wedding is more than material gain, then you will not be disappointed with fewer gifts.

The truth is that your non-traditional wedding day gifts will reflect the true meaning of wedding gift-giving. Your friends and loved ones will give you wedding gifts out of affection, not obligation. They will give gifts because they *want* to and not as compensation for being invited to your wedding. You may even find that you receive nicer, more expensive wedding day gifts when announcing a non-traditional wedding. Friends and family often feel grateful that they don't need to endure the pomp, circumstance, and hassle of attending a traditional wedding and may reward you with better gifts.

While it is very likely that you will receive gifts regardless of the type of wedding you choose, it is important that you don't expect them. Some people may believe that a wedding gift should only be given for a traditional wedding. Others may give you small tokens of congratulations, such as a bottle of champagne or a hand-written note. Accept that you may not receive fancy gifts and don't hold any grudges against those who may not send presents. Remember the reasons you decided to choose a non-traditional wedding and be pleasantly surprised by whatever gifts you receive in honor of your marriage.

If the thought of receiving fewer wedding gifts as a result of choosing a non-traditional wedding is overpowering, then you should definitely go the traditional wedding route. But if you want to discover the true meaning of gift-giving, then definitely think about a non-traditional wedding!

6. Do you and your partner share many similar interests and values?

Choosing a non-traditional wedding offers you and your partner the distinct opportunity to plan a celebration that reflects your individuality. If you prefer to spend your free time in places other than fitting rooms and hotel function halls, then a non-traditional wedding will give you the flexibility to plan a wedding around your interests. Think about what you like to do in your free time. If you both enjoy sailing, plan an adventure wedding on the open seas; if you both love summertime barbecues, plan a surprise backyard cookout for all your friends; if you both enjoy the theatre, consider planning a dinner theatre wedding; if you both ski, get married on the slopes; if you both like reading, get married in your local library; if you both love to travel, consider a destination wedding; and if you both like to save money, elope!

There are no limits on the type of non-traditional wedding you can plan. Decide what you and your partner like to do, and plan your wedding accordingly. Not only will you have a fun and meaningful wedding experience, but you will enjoy the planning and preparation as well.

7. Have you avoided tradition in the past?

If you are a stickler for tradition and ceremony, then a non-traditional wedding may not be right for you. Choosing a non-traditional wedding means breaking from tradition, which can sometimes cause problems. If you have made it this far in the book, then you are probably not opposed to pioneering new ideas. Your family and friends may even expect it of you. Many of the couples interviewed for this book reported that friends and family were not at all surprised by a couple's unique wedding plans. "Deep down the family expected this," said one bride who chose a surprise wedding. If you are comfortable with the thought of challenging tradition and cultural norms, then planning your non-traditional wedding can be a lot of fun. But if you are constantly wondering what others will think of your decision, then you may want to revisit the traditional wedding idea. Whichever wedding option you choose, you should have no regrets.

8. Do you communicate openly with your partner?

Hopefully, you are planning a wedding because you and your partner have a devoted, open relationship based on love, trust, and respect. When planning a non-traditional wedding, these ideals may be tested. Wedding vendors may ignore you, loved ones may be perplexed by you, and colleagues may be indifferent towards you. You and your partner need to make certain that you are both firmly committed to a non-traditional wedding and willing to support each other if tensions mount. Chapter 3 provides some strategies for convincing your spouse that a non-traditional wedding is a great option, but you both need to communicate openly and honestly about your wedding day dreams and expectations.

9. Do you believe that your wedding day is the most important day of your life?

We frequently hear couples (mostly brides) say that their wedding day is the most important day of their lives. While the union between two people who love each other is an extraordinary life event, there are many other moments in life that may be equally exhilarating. Giving birth to a new baby, celebrating a 50th wedding anniversary, accomplishing your ultimate career goal, and successfully overcoming a difficult challenge could all be moments to cherish. If you believe that your wedding day is the pinnacle of your life, with all efforts leading to this one moment, then you should probably plan a traditional wedding to commemorate this day. But if you believe that your wedding is one of many special life occasions, then think further about a non-traditional wedding. If you have many personal and professional goals and numerous opportunities to "shine," then it is probably not essential that you are the center of attention on your wedding day. But if you believe that your wedding day is the only chance for you to be in the spotlight, then definitely plan a traditional wedding.

10. Do your religious beliefs allow you to be flexible with traditions?

It does not need to preclude you from choosing a non-traditional wedding, but strong religious beliefs may steer you toward a more traditional wedding celebration. Many people believe firmly that a wedding is the joining of two people in the eyes of God within a house of worship. For them, a wedding is often a very serious, sacred occasion that should not be tampered with. If you attend your place of worship weekly and you believe resolutely in all the tenets of your religion, then a non-traditional wedding may present too many obstacles and may hinder the sanctity of the occasion. Think about blending a traditional ceremony with a non-traditional wedding reception to create a unique wedding celebration, but also consider if doing so would compromise your religious beliefs.

Many non-traditional wedding couples are very spiritual. They choose a non-traditional wedding to connect more with their faith or the beauty of nature. Non-traditional weddings provide the freedom to express a couple's spirituality and union to each other. Couples frequently weave in vows or customs that reflect their religious or spiritual beliefs. A non-traditional wedding provides the flexibility to express a couple's faith in very meaningful ways, creating a spiritual occasion to be treasured for years. Thinking seriously about your faith and its importance to your wedding day will help you to create a meaningful celebration.

At this point, you probably have a better idea if a non-traditional wedding is right for you. If it is, great! You will have a lot of fun planning your unique wedding. If you have decided that it is not right for you, then seek out resources to plan your traditional wedding day and use this book to balance your traditional customes with your original ideas. If you are still uncertain about a creative wedding option or you would like to blend tradition with a contemporary celebration, then keep reading.

Chapter 3

How to Convince Everyone Else

You're sold on something different for your wedding day, but what about your partner? Or your family? For some of you, the acceptance of family members or friends to your non-traditional wedding may be unimportant. You may be certain that this is what you want to do and don't care what anyone else thinks. If so, skip ahead to the next chapter and start planning. Some of you may only care that your partner is committed to a non-traditional wedding. Others of you may have a list of several family members and friends whom you hope will support your unique wedding plans. For those of you who plan to tell family and friends about your non-traditional wedding and seek their approval, this chapter will offer seven helpful tips on how to persuade your partner or loved ones to embrace an alternative wedding.

1. Let Them Think It's Their Idea

After reading the first few pages of this book, you know without a doubt that you want a non-traditional wedding. You have a list of reasons to share with your spouse or family members on why they should be receptive to a non-traditional wedding. You may be tempted to skip this chapter and move quickly to the planning stage of your

wedding. Resist! To make certain that your unique wedding is a success, it is important that all essential parties are
onboard with the decision and are equally enthusiastic.

The most important, and often most difficult, person to
convince is your partner. You may be covertly reading this
book to conjure up the willpower to confront your partner
about your radical wedding ideas, as your partner is eagerly
planning a traditional wedding. An arsenal of traditional
wedding books, Internet print-outs, and catering menus may
be mounting on your kitchen table and you are looking for
the right moment to invade. Be warned that a frontal at-
tack will not work. Getting your partner to consider and
accept the idea of a unique wedding will take a much more
subtle and well-thought-out strategy.

No one likes to be told what to do or be forced to see
things from a different perspective. Your partner needs to
come to his or her own conclusion that a non-traditional
wedding is the right choice. So how do you get your partner to see the light?

First, bear arms. Be supportive of your partner's traditional wedding planning, but start adding to the kitchen
table pile with non-traditional wedding artillery. Cut out
an article about a surprise wedding. Find a catering menu
for a theme wedding. Send away for a pamphlet on a tropical
destination wedding. Scatter this weaponry around your home,
your partner's home, in the backseat of your car, in your
partner's backpack, and anywhere else where it is likely to be
spotted. When your partner asks about these items, simply
respond that you are really getting into the wedding planning
process and are eager to explore all wedding options.

Next, seize the moment. After you plant the seed for
traditional wedding alternatives and demonstrate your
wedding-planning enthusiasm, watch carefully for your
partner's moment of weakness. This could come at any time,
so be on the look-out and be ready to quickly respond.

Your partner may call you in the middle of the day frustrated by a 45-minute phone call with an unreasonable caterer. Use this moment to suggest that the two of you meet for dinner to talk about this crisis and decide what's really important for your wedding.

Your partner may express annoyance at the absurd suggestions by family members who insist that it is inappropriate to have tulips at a fall wedding. Use this moment as a chance to ask, "Do you think we should be required to follow these traditional wedding rules?" If your partner says no, then begin a discussion about why these rules exist and offer alternatives. For example, you could say that you just read something about a couple who got fed up with the same things your partner is dealing with and decided to look at different types of weddings that would not be so restrictive.

Your partner may be angered by a conversation with his or her mother about the guest list, where the parent demands that certain people be invited that your partner does not know or like. Use this moment to suggest that if you were to pay for your wedding, you might have more control over the guest list and the requirements. For example, you could ask, "Have you thought about planning a wedding where we could be completely in control of the guest list?" When your partner laughs at the impossibility, you could say, "You know, there might be many ways for us to have the wedding that we want and be more in control of the occasion." You might then suggest ideas for a surprise wedding, a theme wedding, or a destination wedding and ask if your partner would be willing to take some time to consider these possibilities.

The key with seizing these moments of weakness (which are likely to emerge in any traditional wedding planning process) is to be calm and non-confrontational. Ask a lot of questions, get your partner talking, and quietly offer alternatives for your partner to think about. If he or she knows you are up to something, you will blow your cover. But if you are patient and supportive, then your partner may begin to be receptive to alternative wedding ideas and may start to embrace the idea of planning a unique wedding.

Many of you may be entirely certain that a non-traditional wedding is right for you and your partner. It's your family and friends who will need persuading. Use the same approach previously described to get your loved ones to think that a non-traditional wedding is their idea. If your best friend is well into the throes of helping you plan your traditional wedding and you want to convince him or her to accept the idea of a non-traditional wedding, send an e-mail with a link to an exotic location and say, "Wouldn't it be fun if all of us flew to the Caribbean and spent a week of wedding celebration there?" This could prompt a discussion about other wedding ideas and show your best friend that his or her involvement in your wedding is paramount.

If you're daring, you could even try some sabotage. For example, you could call your father and tell him that you have found a great photographer for your wedding and all you need is a check for $7,500 as a deposit. If your father begins to object, you could use this as an opportunity to approach the idea of a different kind of wedding that could cost much less.

2. Focus on Their Interests

To convince your partner and loved ones that a non-traditional wedding is the right choice, think about the factors that are driving their traditional wedding planning. What are their top priorities? Your partner may really want to be the center of attention on your wedding. Your future mother-in-law may have her heart set on helping with the wedding planning. Your girlfriends may want to help pick out your wedding dress. Your guy friends may have already planned your bachelor party. Make a list of the traditional wedding factors that are most important to your partner and your loved ones. Then, think about ways that you could approach these loved ones with news of your non-traditional wedding in a way that piques their interests. For example, you could say to your mother-in-law: "The most important thing to me in planning my wedding is that you are deeply involved in the planning process." Now that she's hooked, continue by saying, "Lately, we have been thinking about planning a different type of wedding that is not so focused on traditional rituals. Because we would be creating our own traditions and not following any typical wedding rules, I need your help more than ever in planning this wedding. Do you think you could help me with this?" What mother-in-law would not throw herself at your feet with this statement!

If your girlfriends are eager to help you select your wedding attire, then ask them to help you surf Websites to find ideas for the traditional garb of the location to which you are eloping. Or ask your friends to help you choose which beach to get married on. You will be surprised how often your family members and friends want only to be involved in the wedding planning process. Find ways to focus on their interests and get them excited about your unique wedding planning.

If it is difficult to think about wedding-specific interests that may be influencing your loved ones' desire for a traditional wedding, then think in terms of the common interests we all share: we all want to feel important, we all want more time and more money, we all want less stress and more leisure. Use these universal interests to begin a discussion with family and friends about choosing a non-traditional wedding. You could also think about the specific, personal interests of your loved ones and leverage these interests when building your case for a non-traditional wedding. For example, you could initiate a conversation with your parents focused on both universal and personal interests in the following manner:

"Mom and Dad, we have been thinking a lot about our wedding and have been researching the costs and details associated with a typical wedding ceremony and reception. It looks like the average wedding would cost moew than $20,000 and would take about 250 hours to plan. What we really want for our wedding is to spend time and money on a stress-free wedding with our family. While we haven't come to any decisions because we value your input, we discovered that for less than half the price of a traditional wedding, the four of us and some of our other close family members could fly to Napa Valley and spend a week exploring the vineyards and relaxing in the countryside, while also enjoying an intimate and special wedding ceremony. You have been talking for years about visiting Napa and this seems like the perfect opportunity for us to spend our time and money on a relaxing, intimate wedding celebration. What do you think?"

This conversation focuses on the universal interests of more time and money, a feeling of importance, and less stress and more leisure, while also focusing on the personal interests of certain loved ones. It is presented in a factual, non-threatening way and encourages an open discussion rather than a closed decision. Try this approach with your family members and friends. Consider their specific interests, both wedding-related and personal, and focus on the universal interests all of us share. Becoming "outward-looking" throughout your wedding process will help to persuade others to get excited about a unique wedding.

3. Begin With "Yes" Questions

It is a psychological certainty that if you get people saying yes to your ideas early on in a conversation, it is much more difficult for them to say no later. Salespeople have perfected this tactic. When the telemarketer calls you and asks if you enjoy reading the newspaper on Sundays, and you say yes, it is then more difficult for you to say no to his offer to purchase the Sunday *Times* at a reduced rate.

Use this strategy when approaching your partner or loved ones with your non-traditional wedding ideas. For instance, think about the questions you could ask your partner to which he or she would answer yes and find the right moment amidst the wedding planning to ask those questions. Here is an example of a conversation you might have with your partner if you are trying to get him or her to consider a non-traditional wedding:

Q: Do you think our wedding is primarily about you and me?
A: Yes.

Q: Would you like us to be more in control of our wedding planning, rather than having people tell us what we should do?
A: Yes.

Q: Wouldn't it be nice if we could spend more time together rather than devoting all of our free time to wedding planning?
A: Yes.

Q: Do you want to avoid the time and expense associated with planning a traditional wedding?
A: Yes.

Q: Wouldn't it be fun if we could be more creative with our wedding planning rather than being tied to tradition and customs?
A: Yes.

Q: Could we talk about planning a non-traditional wedding instead?

A: Yes!

Try this strategy on your loved ones as well. Get your friends and family saying yes to your alternative ideas early on and keep them hooked throughout the conversation. For example, you could stage this conversation with some family members about a theme wedding:

Q: Don't you think our wedding is primarily an opportunity for us to have fun and enjoy time with family and friends?

A: Yes.

Q: Don't you think that so many weddings we go to are nearly identical, despite the couple's efforts to make them more personal?

A: Yes.

Q: Wouldn't it be fun to plan something completely different for our wedding that would really involve our guests and keep people engaged?

A: Yes.

Q: Would you be involved in helping us plan a unique wedding?

A: Yes.

Q: Do you like the idea of a unique wedding theme focusing on a murder mystery that would involve all the guests and get everybody laughing?

A: Yes!

Getting your partner or loved ones to say yes to your ideas requires some careful planning, the right moment, and a focus on what's important to them. Think about the wedding option you want and come up with a series of yes-answer questions that will lead your partner or loved ones to believe that this wedding idea makes good sense.

4. Embellish Your Ideas

If you are looking to plan a unique wedding, chances are you're a creative and fun person. Use your cleverness to illustrate the excitement of a non-traditional wedding.

Picture this: Your partner arrives at your home expecting to have an ordinary dinner with you. When he opens the door, he is in for a surprise. You greet your partner in a bikini top with a grass skirt and a flower petal in your hair, and you place a lei around his neck. The dining room is decorated with tiki lamps and majestic sunset photographs. Tropical music plays softly in the background as you and your partner sip pina coladas out of a giant pineapple. You use this creative opportunity to *show* your partner, not tell him, about the romance of a non-traditional tropical wedding. Dramatizing your non-traditional wedding ideas demonstrates your enthusiasm for a unique wedding and can provide an opportunity to discuss traditional wedding alternatives. Your embellishment can also get your partner excited about planning a different kind of wedding.

For your loved ones, try a similar strategy. If you are hoping to plan a casino theme wedding, then invite them on a trip to a casino to begin a discussion about your idea. If you want to show them that a scuba-diving adventure wedding will be great fun, then dress up in full scuba gear and take them through the process of getting married under the sea.

By taking the time to dramatize your ideas and illustrate to your partner or loved ones the excitement of a non-traditional wedding idea, you will engage them in the process. They will likely be inspired by your efforts and devotion to a new idea and may find your enthusiasm to be contagious. You are attracted to a non-traditional wedding because of its fun and excitement. Dramatize these characteristics and get your loved ones hooked!

5. Focus on the Facts

Despite your best efforts to dramatize your non-traditional wedding ideas and focus on the interests of the people about whom you care, you may continue to encounter resistance to your unique wedding. Wedding planning can be very emotional for everyone involved and many of your loved ones may have strong feelings about why a non-traditional wedding would be disastrous. Your job is to focus on the facts. While your loved ones may hate your rationality at first, they may later grow to realize their own mistaken assumptions and may open up to new wedding possibilities.

Here are some of the common emotional reactions to a non-traditional wedding and suggested responses:

Reaction:

If we have a non-traditional wedding,
everyone will be upset.

Response: Ask your partner or loved one who, exactly, will be upset. Make a list of all the people who will be upset at a non-traditional wedding and why they would be upset. You will probably discover that most people will not be upset by a non-traditional wedding. If those who will be upset are very important, then focus on ways to keep them happy but still have a non-traditional wedding. If your partner's father would be devastated if he couldn't walk his daughter down the aisle, then think about a surprise wedding or theme wedding where he would be able to do this. If a sister would be upset by not being the maid of honor, then plan a wedding that would involve her in this role. Thinking rationally about which loved ones would be distressed at the idea of a non-traditional wedding and why will reveal many simple solutions to help you move forward with your wedding planning.

Reaction:
What will the neighbors think?

Response: The social pressure to have a traditional wedding is enormous. Your loved ones may feel the need to "keep up with the Joneses" and not break from tradition. Partners may fear that acquaintances will judge them or ostracize them. Parents may be worried that other people will question their parenting abilities or the values they instilled in their children.

You have several options for responding to these very powerful emotional reactions. The first option is to ask your loved ones why they care about what other people think. Explain that you think this wedding is about two people coming together out of love and commitment, and not about pleasing one's social circle. The second option is to analyze the statistics. You could list the number of friends and family members who had a traditional wedding ceremony and reception and who are now divorced. (If some have been divorced more than once, this could give you extra points!) The third option is to ask the neighbors. If your partner or family member thinks that other people will react harshly to a non-traditional wedding, suggest that you ask these people what they think. Your loved ones will be surprised to learn that most people will be very supportive of a non-traditional wedding.

Reaction:
Everyone has a traditional wedding.

Response: Use the facts presented in Chapter 1 of this book to disprove this argument. Explain that 8 percent of today's weddings are destination weddings. Adventure weddings, theme weddings, and surprise weddings are rapidly becoming popular. And more people than ever before are eloping to far-off places and to their local city halls.

Reaction:
You'll regret it someday.

Response: This is a popular response from family members and friends who think you are making a mistake by not planning a traditional wedding. Respond that while you appreciate their concern and caution, you are committed to a unique wedding. Tell them that if someday you have regrets about avoiding a traditional wedding, then you will go ahead and plan one.

Reaction:
People will think you're pregnant.

Response: In nine months they will know I'm not!

6. Be Willing to Compromise

Any successful negotiation process involves compromise. As you try to persuade your partner or loved ones to support a unique wedding, begin to prioritize your wedding wishes and be prepared for some give-and-take. You and your partner should jot down, in order of importance, the most important features of your wedding day. In this example below, we see that the bride cares most about a white wedding gown, a church ceremony, and a wedding dance, while the groom wants an informal, stress-free, low-cost wedding.

Wedding Priorities	
Bride	**Groom**
1. Formal white wedding gown.	1. No formal traditions.
2. Walking down a church aisle with family and friends watching.	2. Low-stress wedding.
3. First wedding dance.	3. Low-cost wedding.

The couple has some negotiating to do, with the groom perhaps welcoming some traditions and the bride being willing to consider less-traditional wedding day customs. This couple might select a formal wedding ceremony, and then fly to a far-off destination to celebrate a weddingmoon. This couple might also select a theme wedding that could blend a formal ceremony with an inventive reception. Or this couple could choose a private elopement at city hall followed by a traditional church wedding.

Go through the same prioritization and negotiation process with your loved ones. If your family cares most about a big reception and you care most about an intimate ceremony, then plan a private elopement or adventure wedding followed by a celebration party. Openly discuss the most important attributes of your wedding day and be willing to make some creative compromises. Of course, money could hamper your ability to make compromises. If your family is paying for most of the wedding, then they will have more power in deciding the particulars of the day. If you pay for your own wedding, then you will have a much stronger bargaining position.

7. Listen Carefully and Respond Empathetically

Wedding planning is stressful, emotional, and often irrational. The best way to persuade your partner or loved one to consider a non-traditional wedding is to actively listen to his or her problems and concerns and respond empathetically. The following conversation highlights active listening and reflection techniques:

A mother's dream:

"Your father and I have waited our whole lives for the moment to see you walk down the aisle. This will be the most important day of your life and we can't wait to share it with you. Everyone will be there, including the O'Learys, who will fly in from Ireland, and Stefan and Maria, who will travel from Brazil. We will make this an extraordinary occasion! I'll have to go shopping soon for a gown and you'll need to select your reception menu and band. Then we need to design the invitations and buy the wedding favors. Oh, what fun this will be!"

Your response:

"Mom, I am thrilled that you are so happy for us and I, too, am eager for my wedding day. It sounds like this is a moment that you have been waiting for a long time and that you are most eager to get involved in the planning process. I am also delighted that so many family members are willing to travel far distances to see us get married. Is it fair to say that a reception with our family and friends and your close involvement in the wedding planning process are the most important aspects of my wedding to you? If so, then I think we will be able to work together to plan a wedding that creates the wedding you want with the nontraditional elements we are looking for."

Listen carefully and non-judgmentally to the wedding wishes and concerns of your partner or loved ones, restate these wishes and concerns, focus on their priorities, and suggest ways to collaborate and compromise. While conversations may not always go this simply, and factors such as time, money, and family dynamics could challenge you, listening and empathizing can make your loved ones feel important and help you to get your unique wedding.

Planning your unique wedding is a hard lesson in human relations. To get buy-in from your partner or loved ones, you need to understand other people's interests, get them to agree with you, arm yourself with information, and be willing to carefully listen and compromise. Following these seven steps will help you to convince the important people in your life that a non-traditional wedding can be fun, engaging, inclusive, and well received.

Throughout these first few pages, you have learned the meaning of non-traditional weddings and reasons for their increasing popularity. You have also thought carefully about your reasons for wanting a unique wedding and know how to persuade others to your way of thinking. Now it is time to start the planning process. Part II of this book presents a comprehensive non-traditional wedding planner for any type of alternative wedding, and offers resources and suggestions for planning an elopement, destination wedding, surprise wedding, theme wedding, or adventure wedding.

Part 2:
Planning a
Non-Traditional
Wedding

Chapter 4

Step-by-Step Non-Traditional Wedding Planner

Like most couples who choose a non-traditional wedding, you will likely begin your planning in advance to make certain that you achieve the wedding day results for which you hope. Planning a non-traditional wedding can often be difficult because of insufficient information and resources. For instance, the wedding timelines and checklists that appear in most bridal magazines and books are often irrelevant to the unique planning and production of your alternative wedding. In this second part of the book, you will discover a non-traditional wedding planner and timeline, as well as specific wedding planning suggestions for five types of non-traditional weddings: elopements, destination weddings, surprise weddings, theme weddings, and adventure weddings.

Even though each non-traditional wedding option will require a unique plan, the following is a sample timeline that you may find helpful in planning your special celebration. Unlike the elaborate checklists that invade every wedding magazine and planner, the non-traditional wedding planner is customized entirely by you. It can be as elaborate or as simple as you would like, depending on the type of unique wedding you choose. For example, if you choose to tie the knot on the steps of the county courthouse, then there is probably limited planning you will need to do and you can skip to the end of the planner. But, if you decide to plan a Walt Disney World fairy-tale theme wedding with 200 of your closest loved ones, the planning may get a bit more complex. Still, you have the privilege to control your celebration, ensuring that, regardless of the wedding style you choose, planning it will be virtually stress-free!

The beauty of your non-traditional wedding is that you can plan as much or as little as you want. It can be a spur of the moment ceremony during a layover in Vegas, or it can be a surprise extravaganza that you plan for more than a year. In either case, it will be *your* wedding.

This non-traditional wedding planner can help you plan your wedding by highlighting the details and decisions that go into planning any wedding, no matter how small or non-traditional. You will notice that many of the details laid out in this timeline mirror those of a traditional wedding. The difference is in the amount of stress, time, money, and rigidity involved. Selecting your flower arrangement, for example, may consist of picking some tulips from your backyard garden or calling your hotel's wedding coordinator to choose a bouquet of indigenous flora. Ordering your wedding announcements may only involve the click of a button on your computer screen. You may feel that you are going through the motions of a traditional wedding, but your planning will involve much less effort and anxiety.

The planner offers tips for your wedding preparations up to one year prior to your wedding day, but feel free to skip ahead to a later planning time frame if your unique wedding is just around the corner!

6 Months to 1 Year Prior to Your Wedding Day

Be Certain That a Non-Traditional Wedding Is Right for You

While you may be contemplating something a bit different from the traditional wedding ceremony, make certain that you will not go through with wedding day plans that you will later regret. Take one to two months before you start planning the particulars of your day to really wrestle with the idea of an alternative wedding. Perhaps you are already at this stage after reading Part I of this book! Gather as much information as possible about alternative wedding options. Talk to friends and acquaintances who have planned weddings, either traditional or unconventional, and find out what they liked and disliked about their weddings.

In Chapter 2, you asked yourself some important questions to determine if an alternative wedding is right for you. Now is the time to grapple with your answers. If you will be devastated by the thought of not having your father walk you down a church aisle, then a planned elopement or adventure wedding may not be for you. However, a destination wedding with your family or a theme wedding may be delightful choices. Think about the symbols that define a traditional wedding celebration: engagement parties, wedding showers, bachelor parties, first dances, bouquet tosses, cake cutting, best man toasts, bridesmaids and ushers, a long white dress and veil, a sit-down dinner, many guests, and so on. Ask yourself which, if any, of these wedding traditions are important to you and why. During these initial months of planning and contemplation you will determine the wedding choice that is right for you—and it may very well be a traditional wedding. The important thing is to know that you have *chosen* the type of wedding you will have and are comfortable with your decision. It is far better to have reservations and second thoughts before you plan your non-traditional wedding than after.

Decide Which Type of Unique Wedding You Want

Once you have given yourself plenty of time to contemplate a non-traditional wedding and you decide that the excitement and romance of an alternative wedding far outweigh any possible regrets you may have, then you must decide on the type of wedding you want. Perhaps in your month of grappling with the alternative wedding idea, you discovered some aspects of your wedding day that you do not want to sacrifice. For example, maybe you decided that you really can't go through with a secretive plot to marry without your loved ones present. Maybe you determined that your wedding day just wouldn't be complete without a particular aspect of your culture or religion represented. Perhaps you want a formal reception without the traditional ceremony. Or maybe you want a formal ceremony with a non-traditional reception. Any alternative wedding style you choose will be wonderful because *you* have the great privilege to select, plan, and execute your wedding any way you wish.

To customize your non-traditional wedding to meet your expectations, you may decide to gather a select group of family and friends and travel to a country inn or hike a mountain to participate in an intimate and meaningful wedding ceremony. You may decide to have only close friends and family witness a morning wedding ceremony and then hold a large, formal reception for extended family and friends that afternoon. You may decide that you want your wedding day to be exciting and memorable for you and your guests and plan an adventurous white-water-rafting wedding day. Or you may decide on an intimate wedding ceremony on a tropical island, followed by a cocktail party or family reception upon your return. Whatever your decision, contemplating your unique wedding in these first few months should give you a good idea of what will make your special day most meaningful to you.

Determine a Budget

While it is true that choosing an alternative wedding can save you thousands of dollars and hours of aggravation, it is still important for you to establish a budget to keep costs from escalating. (See the sample wedding budget planner on page 62.) The non-traditional wedding option you choose will likely determine the expense of your wedding. For instance, if you decide to pay for 20 family members and friends to travel to Fiji to witness your destination wedding, then your budget will be much larger than if you choose to marry in a small ceremony in your backyard garden.

Choosing a non-traditional wedding will give you more flexibility to decide on which areas of your wedding you would like to splurge without breaking the bank. For example, many non-traditional wedding couples decide to take a first-class honeymoon or purchase more expensive wedding bands, and may select cheaper flowers or self-style their hair. You should decide how much money you want to spend for your wedding and try to stick to it. Traditional wedding costs are often much higher than anticipated, generally costing 10 percent more than expected. Your alternative wedding may cost more than your initial projection as well, but, unlike in a traditional wedding, you have full control over how your money is allocated. This chapter (and those that follow) tries to give you a sense of the price tags associated with each non-traditional wedding purchase. By having access to reasonable estimates of costs for various wedding details, you will be better equipped to create—and stick to—a wedding planning budget.

Non-Traditional Wedding Budget Planner		
Wedding Feature	Your Cost	Average Cost
Reception (including food, liquor, gratuity, cake, and transportation)		$7,630
Engagement rings and wedding bands		$4,877
Photography/videography		$1,814
Wedding attire (including groom's attire and wedding party attire and accessories)		$1,656
Bride's attire, accessories, personal care		$1,523
Flowers		$967
Music		$900
Rehearsal dinner		$875
Other (could include ceremony fees, marriage license, decorations, party favors, and stationery)		$2,118

Decide on a Wedding Location

The versatility associated with a non-traditional wedding allows you to tie the knot virtually anywhere in the world. You may choose to marry at the location where the two of you first met. You may choose a place that has meaning for both of you. You may choose to travel to some distant land for an adventure wedding, or marry in your town common. You may choose to say your "I dos" while parachuting through the air or snorkeling under the sea. You may choose a countryside chapel or a drive-through wedding parlor in Las Vegas. You are free to do what you wish!

Once you have selected your wedding venue, you should research the marriage license requirements of that particular area. Check out the chart on page 96 for detailed information on wedding license requirements for all 50 U.S. States and the District of Columbia, including which states require blood tests, how much the wedding license costs, and if there is a waiting period. For more information on marriage laws by state, visit *www.usmarriagelaws.com*. You will also want to check with the town clerk in the area where you will be married to make your license appointment and confirm license fees and acceptable forms of payment. (Most states require cash-only payment.)

If you decide to marry abroad, you will want to gather information on the legal and cultural requirements of marrying outside of the United States. For example, many countries require you to establish residency in the country in which you are marrying, show your birth certificates and passports, and endure a long waiting period. Your hotel concierge, travel agent or wedding coordinator should be able to direct you to the appropriate wedding resources in the area. There may be more preparation and "red tape" involved in planning an international wedding, but again, the rewards will far outweigh the stresses. The complexity involved in obtaining a marriage license at your wedding location may help to guide your decision of where to marry, but don't let a little extra effort compel you to scrap your dream wedding location. There are plenty of resources to help you, beginning with those found in this book.

Start Making Plans

If your wedding ceremony will be held at a special, off-site location, you will want to make your hotel, function hall, or banquet reservations and purchase airplane or train tickets. It will also be important for you to make initial contact with the site's function coordinator or select your own wedding coordinator to handle the details. Whether you choose a coordinator associated with your hotel or travel venue, or you select an independent wedding coordinator, this person will be able to tell you the availability of the location's wedding/function space and if the facility can accommodate your unique celebration.

Use this inquiry period to get an initial idea of the costs of your unique wedding and the possible locations for your ceremony. Many hotel event planners and wedding coordinators will be able to arrange your marriage license appointment for you; hire a justice of the peace or minister that suits your needs; and reserve photographers, music, flowers, champagne, or anything else you might want. If you will be choosing an adventure or destination wedding, then you should contact the group sales office, or event planner, and begin to gather information on available dates, costs, contracts, and accommodations.

It is a good idea to find out if your hotel, resort, inn, travel agent, wedding coordinator, event planner, or group sales office has accommodated unique or non-traditional wedding ceremonies in the past. If they have, then the planning and execution of your wedding may run more smoothly and easily. If not, then it will be up to you to explain clearly and concisely what type of wedding day you want. You may also need to contact officiants, photographers, florists, and other vendors in the area to make certain that your needs are met. You should not be dissuaded from hosting your ceremony in a location or by a minister not accustomed to such inventive occasions. Just be aware that this choice will require more leg-work, preparation, specificity, and follow-up on your part than you would encounter at a venue which is not new to the alternative wedding scene.

While it may save you some time and aggravation by choosing a wedding venue and vendors who have experience with non-traditional weddings, be aware that it may cost you more money. Often just mentioning the word "wedding" to a vendor will cause the price tag of your non-traditional celebration to grow. If it is feasible, you may want to avoid telling vendors that your event is a wedding celebration. This is particularly good advice if you will be planning a surprise wedding or a theme wedding at a hotel or function facility. Whereas wedding and elopement destinations are accustomed to non-traditional weddings and have reasonable packages for unique couples, hotels and function halls often have set fees for any "wedding" and will quote you a premium rate. Unless you will be asking your wedding vendors to assume most of the planning responsibilities, simply inform your vendor that you are planning a family celebration, tell them what you are looking for in terms of food and entertainment, and ask for a cost estimate. You can tell them you are having a wedding after all fees are finalized and contracts are signed.

If you will be holding your non-traditional ceremony in a backyard garden, public park or beach, or at a friend's house, then you will want to begin to make initial preparations and contacts and decide how you would like your ceremony to run. If you are choosing a more exotic wedding ceremony location, such as marrying atop a ski slope, underwater, or parasailing through the air, now is the time to place some informational calls and make your reservations.

Determine Your Reception Locale

Many non-traditional wedding couples decide to break from tradition and host a reception that is separate from their wedding ceremonies. This is particularly true for couples planning destination weddings or elopements. Your wedding choice may guide your reception choice, or you may choose an entirely different type of reception. Some couples opt to have a reception later in the day following their wedding, either at a banquet halls, friends' houses, restaurants, or their backyards. Other couples decide to host, or have hosted by parents or friends, a reception that occurs after they return from a wedding away. Some couples choose casual, informal wedding receptions; others choose elaborate, formal, black-tie events. Your reception can be a traditional wedding reception, complete with dancing, toasts, photography, and a sit-down meal, or it can be a cocktail hour or Sunday brunch. Should you choose to follow non-traditional wedding etiquette, then it is useful for you to know that receptions that do not immediately follow a wedding ceremony are usually publicized as "celebrations in honor of" your recent marriage.

Whichever reception option you select, it is a good idea to start planning as early as possible. For instance, if you will be having a backyard barbecue with a few close family members and friends, then your planning may be limited. If, instead, you want to host a larger backyard reception, you will want to reserve a tent and a caterer. If your reception will be held at a hall, restaurant or banquet facility, it will be important to book that space as soon as possible. Remember that if you choose a fancy reception, the costs, and stress, can easily climb. Even casual backyard weddings can become expensive. Tent rental and set-up can easily cost several hundred dollars, and it is not unusual for caterers to charge fees of more than $100 per person.

You will want to make sure, at all times, that you are planning an event that *you* want, and not something that you think you need to have. Be careful not to let your wedding reception begin to look like the traditional wedding you chose to avoid! This may become a challenge for you, particularly because so often your loved ones will not quite "get it" that you chose an alternative wedding to avoid the traditional wedding pomp. They may embark on a plan for an elaborate and expensive wedding reception, complete with champagne toasts, a three-layer cake, a multi-piece orchestra, wedding favors, and more. If this is what you want—great! If not, then you need to be assertive about setting parameters and reiterating that *you* are in charge of your wedding, not your relatives. If, of course, the bride or groom's family decides to host a reception in your honor, and will be paying for it, then your reception challenge grows.

When it comes to weddings, money really is power. If your parents or in-laws are paying for any part of your wedding or reception, then it may become more difficult for you to have your say in what goes on. Be certain that you and your spouse are in agreement about what you want for your wedding and reception experience, and then articulate your expectations to your loved ones. If they reject your wishes and continue planning the celebration that they want, then you may need to tell them flatly that they cannot—that you will not participate in a celebration of your wedding that is not right for you. Hopefully, it will not come to this. If you are straightforward with your relatives about your wedding wishes, and if you and your spouse work as a team in expressing these wishes to the family, then you should be able to create a wedding occasion that works well for both you and your loved ones.

Send Out Engagement Announcements

This step is entirely up to you. Many people are excited to announce their engagement and find a formal notification to be appropriate. Some couples choose to publish their engagements in the local newspapers. Many non-traditional couples choose to skip this step altogether. If you decide to not have your wedding plans be a surprise, then you may want to announce the date and location of your wedding. Be warned, however, that when you announce your non-traditional wedding to the world prior to the date, you may be bombarded with opinions, criticisms, and objections that could take away from the personal importance and originality of your wedding day. You also put yourself in danger of a surprise visit from uninvited family and friends should you choose a "private" wedding. You will need to determine if this is a risk you are willing to take.

Many non-traditional wedding couples choose to send out engagement announcements as a way for the couple's parents to demonstrate support for the upcoming union. By having the bride or groom's family, or both, distribute engagement announcements, friends and family will be less likely to think that your decision to have a non-traditional wedding is a whimsical, rebellious, or thoughtless act. The following is sample wording for several types of engagement announcements. Again, this is only a guide. It is up to you to be as original or traditional as you would like.

Engagement announcement issued by the bride's (or groom's) parents:

Mr. and Mrs. Thomas Smith
are pleased to announce the engagement of
their daughter, Lucy Marie, to
Tyson Nicholas McCarthy
Please join us for an engagement celebration
Saturday, the fifteenth of October
Two thousand and five
Fifteen Beacon Street
Boston, MA

Engagement announcement issued by the couple (details not announced):

Lucy Ann Smith
and
Tyson Nicholas McCarthy
are pleased to announce
their marriage intentions

Engagement announcement issued by the couple (details announced):

Lucy Ann Smith
and
Tyson Nicholas McCarthy
are pleased to announce
their engagement

An August wedding in Italy is planned.

Newspaper engagement announcement:

Tyson N. McCarthy (of Cambridge), son of Steven and Candace McCarthy of Golden, Colorado, to Lucy M. Smith (of Newton), daughter of Thomas and Angela Smith of Newton. The wedding is planned for next August.

$ Wedding Planning Price Tag $
Engagement Announcements (100 count)

Traditional engagement announcement stationery and envelopes printed by a stationery store vendor	Estimated Cost: $150
Traditional engagement announcement stationery and envelopes purchased at a stationery store and printed using a laser printer	Estimated Cost: $100
Specialty stationery and envelopes purchased at an office supply store and printed using a laser printer	Estimated Cost: $30
Engagement announcements printed in local newspaper	Estimated Cost: FREE (depending on newspaper)
E-mail announcements or word-of-mouth	Estimated Cost: FREE!

Distribute "Save the Date" Notices

Again, this step depends on the type of wedding you choose. If you decide to have family and friends join you for an adventure wedding, or similar-style weddingmoon, then it is a good idea to send a "Save the Date" notice to these invited guests. This notice can be included with your engagement announcement or sent separately. The notice can be a formal card or an informal letter. It could include information on the type of wedding you are planning; for example, a description of the hiking trail that you and your wedding guests will be backpacking along for your outdoor adventure wedding. It acknowledges that a formal invitation to your celebration will be sent nearer to the wedding date, but encourages your guests to mark their calendars and begin to make travel plans. If your wedding will be far away, include on the "Save the Date" notice a list of nearby hotels and their rates, travel agents, and car rental and airfare information, as well as the date, time, and location of your wedding. Following is a sample "Save the Date" announcement:

SAVE THE DATE!

Carlos & Molly
are excited to announce the
date of their wedding

06.20.2005

Kilcogan Castle
Galway, Ireland

Rooms are available in Galway at:
Radisson SAS Hotel Galway
(800) 333-3333

(Mention the Garcia/O'Shea wedding)

Invitation to follow

4 to 6 Months Prior to Your Wedding Day

Finalize Your Guest List

If you will be having a secretive elopement, then this step is already decided. It will be just the two of you exchanging your vows together in the ceremony and location of your choice. If, on the other hand, you are opting for another type of non-traditional wedding, then you will want to determine whom you would like to invite. If you are planning a faraway destination wedding, then you may be able to invite a lot of people but expect only half to attend. On the other hand, you need to be prepared in the event that everyone decides to travel long distances to see the two of you tie the knot. You will also need to seriously consider the maximum number of attendees, beyond which your unique ceremony will begin to feel more traditional, stressful, and stifling.

Many people find the non-traditional wedding guest list to be the most difficult part of the wedding planning experience because it is easy to encounter numerous "contingency invites," or people whom you feel compelled to invite if you invite someone else. Many couples report that they wanted to have only 10 people present at their wedding ceremony. When they invited these people, however, they were bombarded with criticisms and requests to invite additional family members and friends who "just couldn't be left out." Often couples get stymied at this stage and end up planning a more traditional wedding because of guest-list stress. Be careful not to get caught up in this traditional wedding planning plight at this critical stage. There are many options available to you. Stay focused on making sure that your wedding day will be exactly what you want and with whom you want. Make certain that you and your partner have formed an alliance and are both committed to what your wedding day will entail and who will be present. If you work together as a team, you will be much better prepared to respond to guest-list criticisms and be assertive about your wishes.

Make Your Travel Plans

Make certain that your flights are booked, passports are updated, reservations are made, and deposits are delivered. If your wedding adventure will be combined into your honeymoon, a true weddingmoon, then you will want to ensure that you have made all necessary accommodations, including car rental, marriage license appointments, hair and make-up arrangements, and scuba lessons! If you will be inviting faraway family members to participate in your wedding, check in with them to make sure that they have started making their travel plans.

Decide on Your Wedding Attire

The privilege of being a non-traditional wedding couple means that you are not bound by any rules or customs associated with wedding day dress. Many brides and grooms decide, during their alternative wedding contemplation phases, that they do not want to sacrifice a formal wedding gown and tuxedo. Even secretive elopers who marry on the beach or at a Las Vegas chapel often choose formal wedding attire. Multicultural brides and grooms frequently decide to each wear the traditional wedding dress customary of their individual faith or culture. The choice is yours. If you are going to choose formal wedding attire, then you must start early to find, or make, the dress and suit that are appropriate for you, allowing time for necessary fittings, alterations, and delivery. If you will be marrying away from home, you may want to contact your bridal salon or tuxedo rental store, or your airline, to see about special accommodations that can be made to ensure that your wedding attire arrives at your wedding destination safely and wrinkle-free.

If you are choosing the non-traditional route for your wedding attire, then the possibilities are limitless. You may choose to wear the traditional wedding attire customary of the location at which you are being married. In which case, you should contact local vendors found by searching the Internet or by contacting your hotel wedding coordinator or local tourism bureau. If you choose a theme wedding, then you will want to purchase wedding attire that enhances that theme. If you choose a rock-climbing adventure wedding, then you may choose to wear a pretty, white veil that coordinates with your ropes and harness!

If you would like something less formal than traditional wedding attire, but more formal than your bathing suit or backpacking gear, then it may be helpful to search the Internet and retail stores (even bridal stores), for less formal dress. Bridesmaid dresses can be an especially good choice, as there are often large varieties and colors and they are much cheaper than wedding gowns, averaging about $150. The groom may decide to purchase or rent a nice suit or buy a shirt upon arriving at your wedding destination that reflects the culture and custom of the area. Choosing wedding attire that reflects the originality or your wedding day can help make your wedding more fun and meaningful—not to mention capture in photographs the originality of your wedding day for years to come.

Wedding Attire Online

Best Bridesmaid—Check out *www.bestbridesmaid.com* for a wide selection of affordable dresses that may suit your non-traditional wedding.

Chadwick's—Offers many Web-only deals on wedding gowns and formal wear *www.chadwicks.com*.

ChinaTowner—Looking for authentic Asian dresses? Check out *www.chinatowner.com*.

Cyber Gown—Shop for wedding gowns and formalwear at *www.cybergown.com*.

eBay—Bid for your perfect wedding gown at *www.ebay.com*.

eGowns—Browse through a wide variety of affordable wedding dresses, evening gowns, and bridesmaid dresses available for online purchase at *www.egowns.com*.

Hawaiian Wedding Shop—Find tropical wedding attire for both the bride and groom at *www.hawaiianweddingshop.com*.

Do You Know Where You Will Be Living?

For many couples, not much will change after you say I do. You are perhaps already living together or have settled on the apartment or house that you will be living in when you return as husband and wife. For others of you, now is the time to start contacting Realtors and researching neighborhoods to decide where the two of you will begin your life together.

Notify Your Employer

Let your employer know, as soon as possible, that you will be taking some vacation time in the near future. It will be up to you whether or not to tell your colleagues about your wedding plans. If you are planning an elopement or surprise wedding, you may want to reveal to them your wedding news when they ask how your vacation was! If your wedding won't be a secret, then it may be perfectly fine to share the good news with your colleagues. Just remember that the more people you tell about your non-traditional wedding plans, the greater the likelihood of comments and criticisms.

2 to 4 Months Prior to Your Wedding Day

Finalize Your Wedding Details

Reservations should be made and details nearly finalized a few months prior to your wedding day. Final payments should be sent soon to confirm your travel reservations, ceremony details, caterers, photographers, entertainers, florists, reception or after-wedding dinner reservations, and post-wedding adventures (such as taking a helicopter ride over your tropical island or getting tickets to a Broadway show). You will also want to check in with your event planner, sales office, wedding coordinator, caterer, hotel concierge, or local vendors to confirm that any music, photography, flower arrangements, and so forth, that you have chosen for your ceremony or reception are all set.

If you are choosing a destination or adventure wedding with family and friends, confirm with them that their travel plans are set. If you will be having a wedding party, then you should finalize the details of their wedding attire, flowers, and gifts. If you are planning a rehearsal dinner, then you should make sure that all necessary reservations, payments, and menu selections are finalized.

Purchase Your Wedding Bands

Now is the time for you to visit your local jeweler to purchase and engrave your wedding bands. Of course, if you are planning a last-minute, surprise, or elopement wedding, then you can certainly wait to buy your wedding rings. The more lead time you have before your wedding day, the more certain you will be to get the wedding bands, and other wedding details, that you most want. If you are below budget on the rest of your wedding planning, then you may choose to splurge on your wedding band expenditures. The average traditional wedding couple spends $4,877 on an engagement ring and wedding bands. Many alternative wedding couples report purchasing their wedding bands (excluding a diamond engagement ring) for between $100 and $300. Couples choosing alternative bands, such as an authentic Claddaugh ring for an Irish wedding or a medieval band for a Renaissance wedding, may encounter higher prices and less availability.

Register for Gifts

Because non-traditional weddings have no precedents, it is up to you to decide whether or not to register. Some people might find it presumptuous for non-traditional wedding couples to register. Others want to give you gifts you will enjoy and will appreciate the direction that registering provides. As with the rest of your non-traditional wedding planning, the choice is yours!

To decide whether or not to register, it is a good idea to step back from your own wedding planning and imagine that you received an announcement or invitation from friends who chose a non-traditional wedding. Would you find it odd if the couple decided to register for gifts? If so, then you probably should not register. If not, then go for it!

Some couples choose a middle ground. They don't feel comfortable registering, but they want to help their guests find a useful gift. When someone asks what you want for your wedding, you may say, "Oh, thank you for thinking of us. We decided not to register, but if you're looking for some ideas, we love everything from Crate and Barrel." This way you can direct people to specific shops without registering.

To register or not to register, thankfully, may be the only big decision for you to make when planning your non-traditional wedding. If you decide to register—and many non-traditional couples do—then wedding etiquette recommends that you do not publicize where you are registered. If your guests really want to buy you something that you have chosen for yourself, then they will ask someone close to you where you are registered or check registry lists at popular stores.

Order Wedding Announcements and Invitations

Next it is time to decide on the type of announcements or invitations you would like to purchase. As with all of your non-traditional wedding planning, you have a panoply of options available to you when choosing your wedding announcements and invitations. If your wedding will be a last-minute wedding, a surprise wedding, or an elopement, then your wedding announcement will likely be sent after your marriage to announce to friends and family that you are now married. If you are choosing another type of non-traditional wedding, then you will likely send invitations to your wedding guests and perhaps announcements to acquaintances who will not be participating in your wedding day. Some ideas for wedding announcements and invitations include:

> ➤ You can take the traditional route and have traditional wedding announcements and reception invitations professionally printed at a traditional stationery store.

> ➤ You can visit an online stationery Website to design your announcements and invitations without hassle.

> ➤ You can purchase nice stationery at a traditional stationery store and create your own invitation wording by putting the invitations through your laser printer. (Make sure that the stationery is compatible with your printer.)

> ➤ You can make your own invitations by hand or on the computer, perhaps by scanning in a picture of the two of you or finding an artist friend to create a caricature of you.

> ➤ You can purchase stationery at, or have announcements printed by, a vendor in the location at which you are getting married to add some authenticity and originality to the announcements.

> ➤ You can send free e-mail invitations to friends and family announcing your wedding plans.

> ➤ You can send creative wedding announcements or invitations that capture the originality of your alternative wedding. For example, invitations shaped like sailboats for a wedding at sea, or some plastic sunglasses included with an invitation to a

destination wedding in Jamaica could en-
hance your invitations.

➤   You can decide not to bother with marriage
    announcements at all and simply spread the
    word yourself by making some phone calls.
    This can be especially fun for a last-minute
    wedding or planned elopement when you call
    your friends and relatives via cell phone from
    your wedding destination shortly following
    your wedding ceremony.

As you decide how you would like to announce your
wedding plans, you should again consider what is important and meaningful to you, and not what precedent and
tradition command. If you choose to have your stationery
professionally printed, the costs can mount. Printed announcements, printed reception invitations, outer envelopes, printed reply cards, and printed reply card envelopes
can easily cost more than $500. This may be an area where
you would like to splurge to demonstrate some degree of
formality as you declare your marriage intentions or intro-
duce yourself to the world for the first time as a married
couple. Many non-traditional wedding couples, however,
choose to keep costs down and be more creative with their
wedding stationery.

It is a good idea to visit several stationery stores to get
suggestions for invitation wording, stationery styles, and the
level of attentiveness of the staff. It should not surprise you
to learn that in the volumes of wedding stationery available at stationery stores, only one or two announcements
contain non-traditional wedding wording or offer creative
themes and colorful designs. You may want to search for
your alternative wedding stationery by browsing stationery
samples generally reserved for birthday parties, corporate
functions, family reunions, holiday parties, or other non-
wedding festivities.

Another thing that you may find a bit disheartening during your trip to the stationery store is that salespeople may not be very eager to help you select your stationery upon learning that you are having a non-traditional wedding. They may consider you a poor revenue-generator, and therefore not as valuable as another couple who is planning a large traditional wedding. Or they may not fully understand or appreciate your unique wedding, resulting in an inappropriate level of customer service. If this happens to you, just leave the store. Most stationery stores have the same selections of stationery and you will eventually find a salesperson at another store who is more than willing to help you prepare for your special day.

If you don't find this salesperson, or if you don't want to deal with the hassle involved with visiting a crowded stationery store to wade through volumes of paper, then try the Internet. Many alternative wedding couples find the Web to be the perfect place to purchase their announcements, invitations and thank you notes. Often stationery distributors have their own Websites featuring the same stationery selection found in stores, at half the cost. You can select, design, and pay for your stationery online and have your order delivered the next day!

Online Stationery Vendors

Classy Announcements—Catering to non-traditional couples, this vendor helps you to prepare photos from your unique wedding and incorporate them into creative announcements and invitations. *www.classyannouncements.com*

Colors by Design—This vendor has wonderful non-traditional stationery products and wording suggestions. *www.colorsbydesign.com*

(cont'd)

Crane's Stationery—This large distributor offers many stationery products for you to purchase and fill in on your own. *www.crane.com*

e-Invite—Offers a large variety of custom-printed and blank stationery products. *www.einvite.com*

Evite—Send your wedding announcement or invitation electronically! *www.evite.com*

Fine Stationery—This site has a great selection of stationery to choose from. *www.finestationery.com*

> "I have a friend who eloped in San Francisco. She sent all of her friends a surprise gift. In the box was a split of champagne with an announcement saying she got married and to congratulate her and her husband by toasting. I thought this was the most clever wedding I had ever heard about!"
>
> Check out *www.wine.com* for this creative wedding announcement idea.

There are many options available to you for your announcements and invitations. Be creative and come up with some original ideas. Incorporate some of the culture of your wedding venue, character of your theme wedding, or ethnic flare of a multicultural wedding. Use an unusual stock of paper, send your invitations as a "message in a bottle," mail your announcements with a postmark from your wedding location. The most important thing to remember is that you are not bound by any protocols in announcing your wedding to the world.

$ **Wedding Planning Price Tag** $ **Wedding Announcements and Invitations (100 count)**	
Traditional wedding announcements and invitations printed by a specialty stationery store vendor	Estimated Cost: $325
Traditional wedding announcements and invitations purchased at a stationery store and printed using a laser printer	Estimated Cost: $200
Wedding announcement and invitations purchased online	Estimated Cost: $250
Message in a bottle	Estimated Cost: $20/bottle
Champagne toast announcement	Estimated Cost: $50/person
Newspaper marriage announcement	Estimated Cost: FREE (depending on the newspaper)

The following are some suggestions for wording your wedding announcements and invitations. You may choose to issue your own announcements or have them issued from your parents. The latter choice can help send a message to family and friends that your unique wedding is endorsed by your parents. As with all of your non-traditional wedding planning, the autonomy of your decision-making is based on the assumption that you will be footing the bill for everything. If you choose to accept payment from parents and family, then recognize that your decisions may be more constrained. And finally, if you will be sending after-the-fact announcements of your marriage, always remember to send them after you are *officially* married. You just never know what Murphy's Law may throw your way!

Announcements issued by couple:

Lucy M. Smith

and

Tyson N. McCarthy

are pleased to announce

they were married

Saturday, the nineteenth day of June

Two thousand and four

Kalapaki Beach

Kauai, Hawaii

Announcements issued by parents:

Mr. and Mrs. Thomas Smith

announce with pleasure

the marriage of their daughter

Lucy Marie

to Tyson Nicholas McCarthy

Saturday, the nineteenth day of June

Two thousand and four

Kauai, Hawaii

Newspaper marriage announcement:

Lucy Marie Smith of Newton and Tyson Nicholas McCarthy of Cambridge were married on Kalapaki Beach in Kauai, Hawaii. The bride is the daughter of Thomas and Angela Smith of Newton. A graduate of Brown

University and Harvard Law School, she is an attorney in Boston. The groom is the son of Steven and Alecia McCarthy of Golden, Colorado. A graduate of Princeton University, he is an MBA candidate at Harvard University. The couple lives in Cambridge.

Destination wedding invitation wording (wording will generally depend on who will be paying for the wedding):

Lucy Marie Smith
and
Tyson Nicholas McCarthy
(together with their parents, if appropriate)
request the pleasure of your company
at their wedding
Saturday, the nineteenth day of June
Two Thousand and Four
at six o'clock in the evening
Grand Ballroom
Paris Marriott Champs Elysees Hotel
Paris, France

Adventure wedding invitation wording:

Lucy Marie Smith
and
Tyson Nicholas McCarthy
(together with their parents, if appropriate)
invite you to attend their ski adventure wedding
Saturday, February 5th to Saturday, February 12th
Two Thousand and Two
With a mountaintop ceremony to be held at sunset on
Sunday, February 6th
Vail Mountain Ski Resort
Vail, Colorado

E-mail invitation wording:

Dear Aunt Edna,

Lisa and I will be getting married at the Vail Mountain Ski Resort in Vail, Colorado, on Sunday, February sixth at five o'clock in the evening. We hope that you will be able to join us for the mountaintop ceremony and the informal reception to follow at the ski lodge. Please let us know at your earliest convenience.

Best,

Tyson

Theme wedding invitation wording:

Lucy Marie Smith

and

Tyson Nicholas McCarthy

invite you to attend their Halloween theme wedding

Saturday, the twenty-ninth of October

Two Thousand and Five

Hawthorne Hotel

Salem, Massachusetts

Please arrive in costume!

Surprise (barbecue) wedding invitation wording:

Join us for a summertime barbecue with friends and family

Saturday, July 9th at Noon

Lisa and Tyson's

20 Main Street

Anytown, USA

Please R.S.V.P. by June 25th at: (555) 555-1212

Reception invitations issued by married couple:

Please join us for an authentic New England Clambake
to celebrate our recent marriage
Saturday, June 29, 2002
2:00 - 6:00 p.m.
Please R.S.V.P. by August 1ˢᵗ
617-555-1212, or yourname@aol.com

Reception invitations issued by parents:

Mr. and Mrs. Thomas Smith
invite you to attend a Cocktail Reception
in celebration of (or in honor of)
Lucy and Tyson's marriage
Friday, June 25, 2004
6:00 - 9:00 p.m.
The Downtown Club
Boston, Mass.
Please R.S.V.P. by June 15th
617-555-1212, or yourname@aol.com

Send Wedding Invitations

If you are welcoming friends and family at your non-traditional wedding, then you should mail your wedding invitations approximately eight weeks prior to your wedding day. If you are planning a surprise wedding, then now is the time to call your guests, mail them a casual invitation, or send them an e-mail inviting them to the location of your surprise wedding. If two months prior to your wedding seems too early to invite people to your surprise wedding, then you can certainly wait until the last minute. Just be aware that if you wait too long, many of the people whom you hope will attend your wedding may have other plans.

Like engagement and marriage announcements, your wedding invitations can be sent by either you or your parents, or both. The wording generally depends on who will be paying for the wedding and how traditional the couple wants the invitations to be. Again, feel free to be as informal or formal as you wish in selecting your wedding invitation wording and style.

1 Month Prior to Your Wedding Day

Decide if You Will Change Your Name

Like traditional brides, original brides need to decide whether or not to change their name after they marry. According to Conde Nast Bridal Group Infobank, 83 percent of brides choose to take their husbands' names. (Many non-traditional brides choose to be in the 17 percent minority—must be that whole "property" thing!)

You and your future husband should discuss this decision together to decide what is right for you. If you do decide to change your name, you will want to download the appropriate name change forms from the Social Security Administration, *www.ssa.gov*, as well as contact your local Registry of Motor Vehicles to order a new driver's license. Changing the name on your credit cards, bank accounts, personal memoranda, and at your place of work can be done after you are married, though you may want to inquire now about the process you will need to follow. For example, many banks require that you show your marriage certificate in order to be added to your spouse's bank account or to change your name on your checks.

Attend Bridal Showers and Bachelor/Bachelorette Parties

If your unique wedding is a secret or surprise, then you will probably not partake in any bridal showers or pre-wedding parties. If you are choosing another type of non-traditional wedding, then it is up to you if you would like a shower or bachelor/bachelorette party. Again, you are not bound by the traditional pageantry that characterizes traditional showers and pre-wedding parties. Feel free to create a shower or party experience that is as individual and unique as your wedding will be. For example, if you are planning a masquerade wedding, your shower could serve as an opportunity for your guests to get together and make their costumes!

Create a Wedding Checklist

Begin to create a last-minute, to-do checklist for your wedding. If you need to purchase any accessories for your wedding or your honeymoon, such as belts, jewelry, shoes, make-up, and so on, write those items down. If you are purchasing gifts for your wedding party, now is the time to shop. You may want to purchase some elegant lingerie for your wedding night and will want to remind yourself to go shopping. Write down all important items that you will need to bring with you for your wedding, such as documents for your marriage license and any readings or artifacts you will be incorporating into your ceremony. If you are using a wedding coordinator or other vendors, jot down a note to remind yourself to bring copies of your contracts with you to your wedding location. This way you will have documentation of how your wedding day is supposed to operate in case there is any disagreement. Remember to buy stamps for your wedding announcements and, if you choose to, prepare a marriage announcement for your local newspaper.

Prepare Wedding Vows

Confirm that your marriage officiant is booked and determine how you want your ceremony to be conducted. Will you be writing your own vows, allowing the minister to guide the ceremony as she chooses, or a little bit of both? Now is the time to look through books and on the Web for poetry readings or inspirational passages that will add meaning to your special day. If you have chosen an adventure wedding or theme wedding, then you have probably already notified your officiant of your non-traditional wedding plans. Nonetheless, confirm with your wedding officiant how much flexibility you will have in preparing your ceremony. If you will be inviting family members or friends to read a passage at your wedding, choose the passage now and ask the person if he or she would like to speak.

$ Wedding Planning Price Tag $
Officiant Fees

Average traditional church ceremony	Estimated Cost: $250
Justice of the peace/minister	Estimated Cost: $75
Marriage license and ceremony at city hall	Estimated Cost: $75

Check in With Guests

Once again, check in with any guests who will be attending your wedding, particularly if they will be traveling from afar to attend. If you are planning a theme wedding or adventure wedding, it is particularly important for you to be available to answer questions about what your guests can expect and what, if any, preparations they should make. Confirm that all of their plans are finalized and offer to help in any way that you can. Let them know how happy and grateful you are that they will be participating in your special day—especially if they are paying for their travel expenses.

1 to 2 Weeks Prior to Your Wedding Day

Tell Close Family and Friends About Your Approaching Wedding

If you are planning a surprise wedding, elopement, destination wedding, or a small wedding to which only a few people are invited, then you may decide that now is the time to break the news to a few close friends or family members who you think should have the privilege to know of your plans before everyone else. You have been warned, however, that you need to be discerning about whom you tell and when, forthright about the expectations of your wedding, and resolute in your decision to go ahead with your plans regardless of any negative responses you may receive.

Confirm, Confirm, Confirm

Yes, one last time you need to confirm with your airline, car rental agency, sales office, event planner, wedding coordinator, vendors, hotel, banquet facility, caterer, and so on, that everything is in place and ready for your wedding day. Don't worry about sounding paranoid when you call your florist yet again to make certain that the yellow orchids you ordered will be fresh and fragrant. Vendors are accustomed to staunch follow-up and will appreciate letting you know, again, that all is well.

Get Your Marriage License

A few days prior to your wedding day, you should appear at your prescheduled marriage license appointment where you will likely complete some forms asking for nit-picky information such as your father's middle name, your mother's place of birth, and whether or not you want your names published in the local newspaper. It may be necessary to bring a witness. If either the bride or groom is divorced or widowed, you will be expected to show proof of divorce or death. You will raise your right hand signifying the legal commitment you are about to make and sign your names. If you will be marrying internationally, preparing for your marriage license may take longer than a couple of weeks. You may need to visit the local embassy of the country in which you will be marrying while in the United States to complete paperwork, and then visit the U.S. Embassy in the country in which you will be married just prior to your wedding to complete additional paperwork.

Finalize Wedding Day Plans

You should meet with your wedding coordinator, event planner, and officiant one last time, or perhaps for the first time if you have only spoken by phone, and get a tour of the location at which you will be married. Finalize all details, including rehearsal dinners; hair, make-up or massage appointments; and after-wedding dinner details, to make sure that everything goes according to plan. Or you may decide to change your plans at the last minute.

A non-traditional wedding offers you much flexibility. For example, after spending a week in Kauai and becoming acquainted with the island and its beauty, my husband and I decided the day before we were married to move our wedding from 6 p.m. to 10 a.m. so that we could go for a hike through the lush mountains following our wedding ceremony. We also canceled our prearranged wedding dinner on a private gazebo overlooking the pool in favor of a room-service feast on our oceanfront balcony. Changing our plans at such a late stage was easy to do. The hotel wedding coordinator called the Hawaiian minister and the photographer and asked them to come earlier in the day, and she had no trouble canceling the gazebo dinner. While you will likely stick with your original wedding plans, the flexibility of your non-traditional wedding is just one of the countless benefits of choosing something different for your wedding day. And if you choose a last-minute wedding, it is good to know that very often you can produce a wedding experience that has all of the characteristics you hope for.

The Day Before

Treat Yourself

The day before your wedding, you should treat yourself to something special. Indulge in a manicure, pedicure, round of golf, or couples massage. Purchase an expensive bottle of champagne and enjoy a pre-wedding toast. Take a quiet stroll with your mate or hike a mountain. Visit a museum, sidewalk café, place of worship, or another special place to celebrate your love and capture those precious moments before your wedding day. Even if you will be getting married the following day on the steps of city hall during your lunch hour, take some time to relax and reflect the night before your wedding day.

Enjoy a Rehearsal Dinner

If you are having a formal rehearsal dinner in preparation of your wedding day, then this will occupy most of the day prior to your wedding. But what if it is just the two of you celebrating the day before your private elopement or surprise wedding? Treat *yourselves* to a rehearsal dinner! Make reservations at a romantic restaurant, cook a fancy dinner with expensive champagne, and enjoy a memorable evening prior to your big day.

$ Wedding Planning Price Tag $
Rehearsal Dinner

Average traditional wedding rehearsal dinner   Estimated Cost: $875

"Rehearsal dinner" with just the two of you   Estimated Cost: $150

Your Wedding Day

Do Something Spiritual

By spiritual I don't necessarily mean religious, though this certainly would be appropriate on your wedding day. Do something personal and inspirational on your wedding day. Go for a morning jog with your husband- or wife-to-be. Take a swim in the ocean, a walk through the garden, or a solitary ski run down the mountain slope. Write a note to yourself—or to your partner. Meditate. Reflect. Immerse yourself in the meaning, joy, sacredness, love—*spirit*—of your wedding day.

Ready, Set...

Get your hair and make-up done; put on your wedding attire; gather any flowers or bouquets, vows or passages; and make any final preparations for your ceremony. Don't forget the wedding bands!

Go! Walk Down the Aisle (or Not) and Begin Your New Life Together

Walk down the aisle by yourself or with your father or loved one at your arm, walk hand-in-hand with your beloved, or don't walk down an aisle at all! Gather before an officiant, exchange those precious vows, embrace your new spouse, congratulate yourselves on your unique wedding masterpiece, and frolic away to enjoy your special day.

Call Friends and Family

Many couples who plan an elopement, destination wedding, or adventure wedding decide to break the news of their marriage to family and friends with a phone call shortly following the ceremony. Others will check in with loved ones who were already told of the occasion. A phone call to friends and family from your wedding spot will be forever remembered and appreciated. You should also drop your wedding announcements into the mail now that your marriage is official!

A Toast to Your Love and Happiness!

Congratulations on planning and executing your unique wedding! Cheers to you as you begin your new life together!

This chapter provided a model timeline for planning your unique wedding. Depending on the type of non-traditional wedding you choose, your planning time frame and obstacles may differ. The following chapters guide you through a more in-depth analysis of five specific non-traditional wedding options and their unique planning challenges. If you already know the type of alternative wedding you want, then feel free to skip ahead to that chapter. If you are still undecided, then read on to learn more about planning an elopement, a destination wedding, a surprise wedding, a theme wedding, or an adventure wedding. The subsequent pages will help you to choose and plan an alternative wedding experience that is meaningful, enjoyable, uncomplicated, and right for you.

Obtaining a Marriage License by U.S. State

U.S. State	ID Requirement*	Waiting period?	Blood test?	Cost**
Alabama	Valid driver's license or birth certificate	No	No	$30.00
	and Social Security number	3 days	No	$25.00
Alaska	Photo ID; Marriage license application must be notarized			
Arizona	Valid driver's license or ID with current address and date of birth and a certified copy of birth certificate	No	No	$50.00
Arkansas	Photo ID and birth certificate	No	No	$35.00
California	Photo ID and birth certificate	No	No	$80.00
Colorado	Government-issued photo ID or birth certificate and	No	No	$10.00
	Social Security number	No	No	$10.00
Connecticut	Government-issued photo ID or birth certificate and Social Security number	No	No	$35.00
Delaware	Valid driver's license or birth certificate, and Social Security number	24 hrs. residents; 4 days otherwise	No	$35.00
District of Columbia	Valid driver's license and certified copy of birth certificate	5 days	Yes	$45.00
Florida	Valid driver's license or birth certificate, and Social Security number	3 days residents; none otherwise	No	$88.50
Georgia	Two forms of government-issued identification	No	No	$26.00

Hawaii	Two forms of government-issued identification	No	No	$50.00
Idaho	Valid driver's license and birth certificate	No	No	$28.00
Illinois	Government-issued ID card	1 day	No	$30.00
Indiana	Valid driver's license or government-issued ID with current address and date of birth	No	Yes (for brides under age 50)	$18 residents; $60 otherwise
Iowa	Photo ID and Social Security number	3 days	Yes (for brides under age 50)	$30
Kansas	Certified copy of birth certificate	3 days	No	$75
Kentucky	Photo ID and Social Security card or birth certificate	No	No	$34.50
Louisiana	Certified copy of birth certificate, and Social Security number	72 hours	No	$25
Maine	Photo ID and Social Security number	3 days	No	$37
Maryland	Driver's license and birth certificate	2 days	No	$35
Massachusetts	Photo ID and Social Security number	3 days	Yes	$4
Michigan	Certified birth certificate, photo ID, and Social Security number	3 days	No	$20 for residents; $30 otherwise
Minnesota	Photo ID and Social Security number	5 days	No	$70
Mississippi	Photo ID and Social Security number	No	Yes	$22
Missouri	Photo ID and Social Security number	3 days	No	$50
Montana	Photo ID and certified copy of birth certificate	3 days	Yes (bride)	$30.25
Nebraska	Photo ID and Social Security number	No	No	$15
Nevada	Government-issue ID card and Social Security number	No	No	$34-42 (depends on county)
New Hampshire	Government-issue ID card and Social Security number	3 days	No	$45
New Jersey	Photo ID and, in some counties, proof of residency	3 days	No	$28
New Mexico	Photo ID or birth certificate and Social Security number	No	No	$40
New York	Government-issued ID card	24 hours	No	$25-$30

New York	Government-issued ID card	24 hours	No	$25-30
North Carolina	Photo ID or certified copy of birth certificate and Social Security number	No	No	$50
North Dakota	Photo ID and certified copy of birth certificate	No	No	$35
Ohio	Government-issued ID card and Social Security number	No	No	$40
Oklahoma	Driver's license or certified copy of birth certificate or Passport and Social Security number	No	Yes	$25
Oregon	Driver's license or certified copy of birth certificate or passport and Social Security number	3 days	No	$60
Pennsylvania	Valid driver's license and Social Security number	3 days	No	$40
Rhode Island	Certified copy birth certificate	No	No	$24
South Carolina	Valid driver's license and Social Security number	24 hours	No	$15
South Dakota	Valid driver's license or certified copy of birth certificate	No	No	$40
Tennessee	Valid driver's license or certified copy of birth certificate or valid passport and Social Security number	No	No	$95
Texas	Valid driver's license or government-issued ID, and certified copy of birth certificate and Social Security number	72 hours	No	$36
Utah	Valid photo ID and certified copy birth certificate and Social Security number	No	No	$45
Vermont	Valid photo ID and certified copy of birth certificate	No	No	$20
Virginia	Valid photo ID and certified copy of birth certificate	No	No	$30
Washington	Valid driver's license or certified copy of birth certificate or valid passport	3 days	No	$52
West Virginia	Government-issued ID card; proof of age	No	No	$30

| Wisconsin | Social Security number and certifiedcopy of birth certificate | 5 days | No | $80 (waived for additional $10 fee) |
| Wyoming | Valid driver's license and certified copy of birth certificate and Social Security number | No | No | $25 |

* Most states also require proof of divorce or death prior to issuing a marriage license.

** Most states require payment in cash for marriage license fees. License fees often vary by city, town, and county. Check with the local marriage clerk's office for updated marriage license fee information.

Unique Wedding Checklist

6 Months to 1 Year Prior to Your Wedding Day

___ Make certain that a non-traditional wedding is right for you.

___ Choose the type of unique wedding you want.

___ Decide on a budget.

___ Choose a wedding location/reception venue.

___ Make initial wedding/reception/travel reservations.

___ Send out engagement announcements.

___ Distribute "Save the Date" notices.

4 to 6 Months Prior

___ Finalize your guest list.

___ Make your travel/honeymoon reservations.

___ Purchase your wedding attire.

___ Decide where you will live after the wedding.

___ Notify your employers.

2 to 4 Months Prior

__ Finalize your wedding reservations and details.

__ Purchase your wedding bands.

__ Register for gifts.

__ Order wedding announcements and invitations.

__ Send wedding invitations.

1 Month Prior

__ Decide if you will change your name.

__ Attend bridal showers and bachelor/bachelorette parties.

__ Create a last-minute wedding checklist.

__ Write wedding vows.

__ Check in with guests.

1 to 2 Weeks Prior

__ Share news of a surprise or elopement wedding with select loved ones.

__ Confirm, confirm, confirm.

__ Get your marriage license.

__ Finalize wedding day plans.

The Day Before

__ Treat yourself.

__ Enjoy a rehearsal dinner.

__ Do something spiritual.

Your Wedding Day

__ Go for it!

Chapter 5

Elopements

Perhaps you have started to plan a traditional wedding and while perusing through the bookstore for traditional wedding guides, you stumbled across this book at just the right moment when you long to run away, get married, and avoid the stress of planning your traditional wedding. For others of you, a romantic elopement may be something you have dreamed about for many years and you want some tips on how to plan such an endeavor. Still others of you may be exploring the many varieties of non-traditional weddings and hoping to learn more about this quintessential non-traditional wedding option. Whether you are wistfully hoping to escape traditional wedding planning or have planned on eloping for quite some time, this chapter will offer you everything you need to know to plan your elopement.

You may want to plan an elopement if:

> You and your partner want to get married alone.

> You want to be entirely in control of your wedding day.

> You want your wedding ceremony to be a relaxed, private moment.

> You want to avoid opinions from friends and family.
> You want to get married soon.
> You are flexible.
> You want to combine a wedding and a vacation.
> You want minimal planning and stress.
> You want to save money.
> You want to combine a private ceremony with a post-wedding celebration.
> You can keep a secret!

For years, many couples believed that their only two wedding options were to have a traditional wedding or to elope. Eloping was reserved for rebellious couples who wanted to escape from disapproving family members, get married spontaneously, or avoid an out-of-wedlock pregnancy. Today, couples choose an elopement wedding for a variety of reasons, few of which are tied to age-old stereotypes. Yet, the myths of eloping remain. To set the record straight about eloping, and offer you planning steps for your special elopement, let's explore the seven most common elopement myths.

Myth #1: Elopements Are Planned at the Last Minute

While some couples still fly off for an impulsive, drive-through Las Vegas elopement, most of today's elopers are much more calculating with their wedding plans. At the Little Chapel of the Flowers in Las Vegas, for example, 75 percent of the chapel's 7,000 weddings performed each year are planned months—up to one year—in advance. As you begin your elopement planning, your first step should be to ensure that this is the right wedding option for you. While nearly every engaged couple engrossed in traditional wedding planning toys with the idea of eloping, there are some significant trade-offs to consider. Of course, you will have a relaxed wedding planning process and wedding ceremony. You will enjoy many private moments with your partner. You will save money and maintain control of your wedding day. You can plan your wedding any time, anywhere. You can celebrate later with family and friends.

These benefits are enticing, but they are also off-set by some considerable drawbacks. Family members and friends are influenced by stereotypical images of elopements and can be devastated with the news of your elopement. They may urge you to plan a "real" wedding later so that they can save face in their social circles and be involved in your wedding experience. Elopements can also be frustrating when dealing with unsupportive wedding vendors inexperienced in elopement weddings. The fact that your elopement may not be a wedding vendor's top priority may also require you to be more organized, persistent, and certain about what wedding details you want. Elopements also require creative, independent thinking. Traditional wedding stores and resources are insufficient for an eloper's unique needs and you will need to take the time to explore non-wedding resources when planning your elopement. Finally, elopements can spin out of control if too many people learn of your plans before your wedding day.

You and your partner should think seriously about these trade-offs in the early days of planning an elopement and make certain that this unique wedding is absolutely what you want.

Elopement Trade-Offs

Pros	Cons
They are relaxed and care-free.	They can cause family upsets.
They can be inexpensive compared to traditional weddings.	They can lead to frustration when dealing with certain wedding vendors.
They allow you to maintain full control of your wedding day.	They require independent, out-of-the-box thinking.
They are planned as a couple.	They can require a lot of organization and follow-up.
They can occur anywhere in the world, at any time.	They can lead to aggravations and unwelcome opinions if too many people learn about the elopement prior to its occurrence.
They can be followed by a hassle-free, post-wedding celebration.	They conjure up many unwanted stereotypes.

Myth #2: Elopements Are Held in a Courthouse

Courthouse weddings remain popular for many couples, but more and more eloping couples choose a romantic destination for their wedding to indulge in a luxurious wedding vacation. After you decide to plan an elopement, start talking about where you would like to get married. Popular wedding destinations, such as Hawaii, Florida, Las Vegas, and the Caribbean Islands, cater to romantic elopements and offer reasonably priced, all-inclusive elopement packages. If a tropical island is not quite what you are looking for, consider traveling to a country inn that has experience with small weddings and access to a wedding officiant. If you want something more adventurous, embark on a cruise ship! Most of the major cruise lines accommodate elopement weddings and destination weddings and allow you the special opportunity to get married by the captain of the ship in the open seas.

For a "traditional" elopement experience, fly away to Scotland and get married at Gretna Green. The fabled Gretna Green is a small town on the Scottish border that couples eloped to beginning in 1754 after strict marriage laws were passed in England and Wales. More than 4,000 couples travel each year to Gretna Green for a care-free wedding that is solemnized with the clank of a blacksmith's anvil, a tribute to the Gretna Green blacksmiths who performed the elopement ceremonies in the 18th and 19th centuries. (Visit *www.gretnagreen.co.uk* for more information.)

While this book cautions against notifying wedding vendors about your unique wedding plans due to the high fees that the term "wedding" often fuels, when planning an elopement wedding it is a good idea to choose wedding destinations that have experience in this wedding option. Finding a hotel, inn, cruise ship, or other venue that welcomes small weddings and elopements can make your wedding planning more enjoyable and stress-free. Nothing can dampen your day as much as contacting a wedding vendor about your wedding plans and hearing the scorn in the representative's voice when you say that you are planning an elopement. If a location is accustomed to planning traditional weddings, it's likely that you won't receive the level of service and respect you deserve when preparing your non-traditional wedding.

Visit Websites of your favorite destination spots and contact the wedding coordinators at that location to find out how accommodating the vendors will be to your wedding plans. Included in this chapter is a list of hotels, inns, and bed-and-breakfasts by U.S. state that cater to eloping couples. Certain locations have more to offer elopers than others, with Arkansas, California, Colorado, Louisiana, Nevada, and Vermont leading the pack in intimate wedding accommodations. Be sure to ask for references from other couples who have planned elopements or small weddings at these locations.

If you locate an elopement destination that will cater to your every need, then your remaining planning steps will be minimal. Most function coordinators or wedding planners who work with elopers will handle all of your wedding details, from ordering your flowers, to booking your marriage license appointment, to reserving an officiant that suits your needs. If you decide to handle most of the details on your own, be aware of wedding vendor resistance. Many eloping couples tell tales of walking into a floral shop to order a "small" wedding bouquet only to be barraged with floral books and wedding bouquet options that start at several hundred dollars.

When you plan an elopement wedding, you will find that you won't get the hand-holding and coddling from vendors that you would if you were planning a traditional wedding. You should be very clear about which wedding details you are looking for and carefully consider whether or not you need to say that you are looking for a "wedding" purchase.

You also need to "think out of the box" when planning your elopement. For example, if you really want to elope to New York City but can't find a hotel to accommodate your wedding, then consider finding your own officiant and then taking advantage of one of the "Romance" or "Honeymoon" packages that many hotels offer. For example, the Four Seasons Hotel in New York City offers a "Romance and Style" package that includes luxurious accommodations, chocolate-covered strawberries and champagne, and breakfast—the perfect place to celebrate your elopement.

You may also want to think creatively when finalizing other wedding details. If you decide to purchase wedding announcements or invitations at a local stationery store for a post-wedding celebration, you may want to avoid the wedding stationery books and instead search in the books that are focused on parties or other non-wedding occasions. Similarly, you may want to avoid bridal stores when purchasing your wedding attire. Consider purchasing an authentic dress or outfit at your wedding destination, searching local department stores for a simple white gown or suit, renting wedding attire, or using Internet resources. By avoiding traditional bridal shops, you will save yourself money and aggravation.

Myth #3: Elopements Are Secretive

Webster's dictionary definition of "elope" is: "to run away secretly with the intention of getting married, usually without parental consent." Well, Webster is wrong. Today's elopers often tell parents or other loved ones of their plans prior to their wedding day. After you decide that an elopement is right for you and you select your elopement destination, consider whom you should tell about your approaching nuptials. Some elopers choose to tell a close friend or family member who will be supportive of their plans and can help them with any last-minute details. Some elopers tell everyone of their plans and some choose to not disclose their plans to anyone at all. As you decide whom to tell, be aware of the following hazards:

1. The more people you tell, the more control you lose.

When you disclose your elopement—even to your most loyal friend—you need to be prepared that the news may get out. As loved ones discover your covert plans, they may try desperately to convince you not to plan an elopement or may be so disappointed at your intentions that the excitement and romanticism of your plans is diminished. Be very careful about whom you tell of your plans and how you will cope with negative reactions, should they arise.

2. The order in which you tell people can be significant.

If a brother learns of your plans before a sister, or one friend is told before another, emotions can escalate. When you choose to tell people of your elopement plans prior to your wedding day, you are granting certain people privileges that others do not have. Some loved ones may feel hurt that others learned of your plans before they did and this could lead to family upsets and fractured friendships. Think about your family dynamics and the strength of your friendships and make sure you are strategic about when you tell certain people of your plans.

3. Secrets can be a burden for the keeper.

As with any secret, it can be difficult to lie or deceive others. When you tell your family members and friends of your secretive plans, be aware of the burden you are asking them to assume. It may be difficult for your loved ones to dodge questions about your wedding or keep your plans a secret. This is particularly true if you decided to elope amidst planning a traditional wedding. Loved ones may be asked questions about your approaching wedding, and will need to find ways to avoid answering these questions. Be respectful of the burden you are placing on your loved ones to keep your secret.

Myth #4: Elopements Are Sterile, Civil Ceremonies

The fourth myth of elopements is that they involve cold, mechanical ceremonies that are impersonal and unmemorable. In fact, elopement ceremonies can be very meaningful and spiritual and are tailored almost entirely by the eloping couple. If you choose a wedding destination that has experience with elopements and weddings, your destination wedding coordinator will likely have several officiants from which you can choose, depending on the type of service you are seeking. Many exotic locations even provide an opportunity for you to get married by a native officiant, such as a Buddhist monk in Bali or a Hawaiian minister in Maui. These exotic ceremonies can incorporate native language and customs which can add to a magical elopement service. Many eloping couples also choose to write their own vows or incorporate personalized exchanges into the ceremony. Most officiants will accommodate your wishes, but be sure to check with the officiant or your wedding coordinator beforehand.

Elopement ceremonies are far from impersonal rites. They can be beautiful celebrations that incorporate meaningful sayings, spiritual beliefs, and native customs.

Myth #5: Elopements Are Rejected by Loved Ones

Family disappointment to your elopement can certainly be a significant drawback, but, unlike popular belief, most of your loved ones will wholeheartedly embrace and support your elopement decision. Immediate reactions to your unique wedding will likely be varied, but many of your friends and family members will tell you how romantic your elopement sounds and will quietly disclose that they wish they had planned an elopement wedding. Nevertheless, be prepared for negative reactions. Explain your reasons for choosing a non-traditional wedding and show compassion for your loved ones who may feel deceived or ignored. For those loved ones who eagerly accept your elopement decision, shower them with gratitude and express how much their support means to you.

When planning your elopement, you should definitely be prepared for negative family reactions and some surprising responses from your loved ones. But you should also take heart in knowing that the majority of your friends and family will be delighted by the news of your unique wedding.

Myth #6: Elopements Are Isolated Events That Don't Involve Loved Ones

Many elopers still choose to plan their wedding in total secrecy and announce their new marital status when they return from the elopement destination. But more and more couples are turning their elopement into a family affair. While an elopement is defined as a wedding ceremony with just you and your partner present, your family can be included in as much of the wedding preparation process as you wish. Many elopers who tell certain loved ones of their plans enjoy the help they receive from a mother who assists in designing the marriage announcements, a brother who throws a small bachelor party, or a sister who helps select the wedding attire. Supportive loved ones can also help to defend your unique wedding to others who may be less than enthusiastic.

Should you choose to keep your elopement a complete secret, your family and friends can still be involved in your wedding celebration after the elopement. Most elopers plan some type of post-wedding celebration to commemorate their wedding and welcome their loved ones into their new married life. Family and friends can be instrumental in helping to prepare a post-wedding celebration. Just be certain that you lay the ground rules, if any, to avoid turning your post-wedding celebration into a traditional wedding day.

Myth #7: Elopement Weddings Don't Last

One of the most common reactions to elopement weddings is, "That wedding won't last." With the majority of today's engaged couples more focused on their wedding day than their marriage, elopers have a distinct advantage. You have the privilege of planning your elopement wedding as a couple and are likely choosing to elope because you want to say I do in a relaxed, private setting. You share similar values and beliefs and care more about each other than about what others think. You are strong, independent, and creative and the odds are good that you will avoid the fate of half of today's married couples and live happily ever after.

> "My husband and I eloped after we started to plan our traditional wedding and the stress that this put on our relationship was too much. We decided to elope and we were much happier.
>
> "If you love each other then it doesn't matter how you exchange the ring: it can either cost you a few hundred dollars or several thousand. My wedding cost $400 total and we put the $15,000 it would have cost for the wedding as a deposit on our house.
>
> "We have been happily married for five years and have a beautiful son."

Unique Wedding Spotlight:
Dave & Jen's Tropical Elopement

David and Jennifer Howard chose to plan a tropical elopement to save their large and scattered family members the logistical and financial burden of traveling great distances to watch the couple wed. Dave is originally from Scotland, where most of his family members still reside, while most of Jen's family lives in the United States. The couple realized that a traditional wedding would have caused unnecessary stress for everyone involved, so they decided to seek alternative wedding options.

Here is the 10-step plan they followed to plan their tropical elopement:

Step 1. Decide when you want to get married.

Jen and Dave decided that they wanted to get married within a year. Jen had already bought her dress while looking at dresses to wear to a friend's wedding, and the couple wanted to give plenty of notice to their employers.

Step 2. Choose your elopement destination.

In their seven years of dating, the couple had never taken a "tropical vacation." They decided to find a place where they could be married while also enjoying an exotic vacation. They narrowed down their marriage/vacation destination by reading Caribbean travel books, browsing the Internet, and asking friends about places they really enjoyed and would return to. Ultimately, the couple chose to marry in St. John.

Step 3. Decide what else you want to do at your elopement destination.

The couple made a list of what else they wanted to do, *after* the marriage ceremony. Being married was a top priority, and the entire reason for the trip, but they also wanted to enjoy a tropical vacation. "We decided to get married within the first few days of the vacation, rather than waiting in anticipation and flying home soon after the ceremony," said Jen.

Step 4. Make travel arrangements.

After reading up on the Caribbean, Jen and Dave found that they could cut costs by traveling in the fall, the tropical off-season. Also, flying out midweek greatly reduced the airfare. Six months prior to their wedding, they met with a travel agent and booked their nine-day tropical excursion.

Step 5. Decide on wedding day details.

Even before they booked the flights, Jen and Dave knew that they wanted to be married on a beach. They investigated the beaches in St. John and came up with three beaches that were enticing. Then, they needed to finalize other wedding details. Who was going to marry them? Did they want just a justice of the peace? Who were going to be their witnesses? What about a photographer and videographer?

At this point, the couple started getting overwhelmed. "We would have to research and interview vendors who were 3,000 miles away! Then, we discovered several wedding companies that could take the hassle out of this. They offered various wedding sites and packages. We printed off three of the companies from the Internet, compared prices, and narrowed it down from there. Before we knew it, we were making arrangements with a very professional young woman from St. Thomas," said Jen. Their wedding coordinator provided helpful advice, and was able to tailor her services to the couple's specific needs. She also handled all of the legal aspects of the offshore wedding. In less than a month, the couple confirmed the wedding date, location, time, officiant, and contractual agreement.

Step 6. Plan a post-elopement celebration(s).

Jen and Dave decided that they wanted to throw a celebration for family members living in the United States shortly after their return from St. John. Planning the party was the most time-consuming part of their elopement journey. It had to be on a weekend due to everyone's busy schedules, and they needed to have it in a hotel for those who wished to stay over.

Three months prior to the elopement, the couple met with several banquet managers. "Because we were looking for a wedding reception in late fall, we thought we could find some deals, but were disappointed that wedding costs remained the same regardless of the season," said Jen. They probably should not have told the banquet managers they were planning a *wedding* reception!

After persevering, the couple finally found a supportive hotel banquet manager who was able to work within their budget and design an evening that met their needs. The manager also provided Jen and Dave with an extensive list of local DJs and bands and, after a few screening phone calls, they found someone with the experience and enthusiasm they were looking for.

The final reception detail to finalize was the flowers. Originally, the couple had their hearts set on a very large vendor situated within walking distance of the hotel. After repeated efforts to contact the florist, and a lack of professionalism in the response, they decided to look elsewhere. They asked for suggestions from colleagues and quickly found a vendor who took the time they needed to go over cost, transportation, and floral design. It was a little more money than the couple had wanted to spend, but the peace of mind and professionalism made it all worth it.

Step 7. Send wedding announcements/ reception invitations.

Jen and Dave made their reception attendee list and sent out invitations about six weeks prior to their wedding. In the invitations, guests who did not already know learned about the planned elopement and the reception that would follow after the couple returned. Their family helped tremendously with the invitation process, including gathering addresses, writing out the envelopes, and coordinating ordering and mailing arrangements.

Step 8. Prepare for the wedding ceremony.

The couple awoke to a balmy 80-degree day in the Virgin Islands. They ate a big breakfast, then rented a car and some snorkel gear, and headed out for some island touring. Later that morning, they drove to the beach where they would be married that evening and selected the spot where they wanted to marry.

With only four hours to go, the couple enjoyed a nice lunch at one of the local eateries overlooking the bay. Jen met with the stylist an hour later, for hair and makeup. The couple returned to the resort to don their wedding attire. The trip to the ceremony was relaxing and stress-free, except for dealing with a few donkeys crossing the road!

Step 9. Exchange vows.

Jen and Dave met their wedding coordinator, minister, videographer, and photographer at 5 p.m. They chatted briefly about the day and the couple's relationship, then started the ceremony. "Other than a rambunctious dog running freely on the beach and the island mosquitoes, the moment was spectacular. We could not have imagined a more glorious evening," said Jen.

Step 10. Enjoy your elopement "reception."

After the ceremony, the newlyweds regrouped at the resort, called their parents, and went to dinner at an ocean-front Italian restaurant. They then celebrated the night away with an evening of reggae dancing to local calypso music.

Dealing with the elopement aftermath.

Jen and Dave's family and friends were very supportive of their non-traditional wedding. The couple was engaged for three-and-a-half years, and family members were ecstatic that they were finally getting married. Family and friends told the couple all along to do what they wanted to do, so that encouragement helped to validate their final decision.

There may, however, be certain unanticipated emotions that appear in the aftermath of an elopement that couples considering this unique wedding option should be aware of. As Jen recalled:

"The day after we were married in St. John, it hit us both very hard that only we could truly know what our wedding day was like. We spent it with strangers, those in the business of marrying couples and the locals who reside on the island. We were sitting by the pool the evening after our wedding and our emotions took hold. Our parents weren't there to participate in what was also their most joyous time. Sure, we had a video, but it could never replace the actual experience. Sure, we could frame a beautiful picture of us in our wedding attire, but those in our life that we love so much couldn't be there to help ease the day's jitters and celebrate the day's finale. That was the emotional reality of our non-traditional wedding."

Tips for Other Eloping Couples

1. With your budget in mind, it makes a lot of sense to explore your elopement options. Try to find a location that can give you inclusive meals or discounted car rentals. You could end up over budget if you have to pay for every meal, every day.

2. Find professionals in the business. Shop around! Get referrals! It takes a lot of trust to allow people to coordinate and manage the fine details of your elopement wedding, especially when you rarely have a chance to meet your vendors prior to your wedding day. Trust yourself and your partner. If something doesn't seem right, don't accept it. Ask as many questions as possible. Demand a 24-hour turnaround time on communication. Get invoices and receipts. If you are relying heavily on the Internet, make sure the Website has testimonials or references. Go a step further and call the local chamber of commerce to make sure the vendor is in good standing.

3. Stay in control by staying organized. Keep spreadsheets of what has been spent, what is owed, and when. Store all vendor contact information for future reference. Keep a file with all your notes, invoices, and ideas.

$ Jen and Dave's Island Elopement Details $

Air fare	= $800 roundtrip
Hotel	= $2,500 for 8 nights
Officiant	= $100 charitable donation in lieu of payment
Wedding coordinator (including photographer and officiant)	= $1,000
Elopement day flowers	= $90
Videographer	= $250
Wedding gown and accessories	= $175
Wedding day hair and make-up	= $125

(cont'd)

Groom's attire (new shirt and sport coat)	= $550
Wedding announcements/invitations	= $300
Post-elopement reception	= $5,000
Total elopement costs (excluding reception)	= $5,890
Total planning time	= 7 Months

Tropical Elopement Resources
Aruba
Aruba Tourism Site—Resources and information for visiting the island of Aruba. *www.aruba.com*
Bermuda
Bermuda Department of Tourism—Information on getting married in Bermuda. *http://www.bermudatourism.com/*
Cayman Islands
Cayman Islands Department of Tourism—Information and resources to help you plan an elopement to this tropical paradise. *www.caymanislands.ky/services/weddings.asp*
Hawaii
Department of Health—Learn how and where to obtain a marriage license. *www.hawaii.gov*
Hawaii Visitors & Convention Bureau—Links to wedding resources on each of Hawaii's islands. *www.gohawaii.com*
Tahiti
Tahiti Tourism Website—Helpful information and links on traveling to and marrying in Tahiti. *www.tahiti-tourisme.pf*
United States Virgin Islands (USVI)
USVI Tourism Department—Download the USVI wedding guide for information on legal requirements and links to island wedding resources. *www.usvitourism.vi*

Unique Wedding Spotlight:
John and Christina's Las Vegas Elopement

What elopement resource guide would be complete without information on planning a true Las Vegas, spur-of-the-moment elopement? John and Christina Scalcione joined ranks with hundreds of thousands of couples when they planned their Las Vegas wedding. John was at a business convention in Las Vegas in October 2002 and Christina flew out to meet him for a couple of days. They thought the trip would only entail visiting the city's famous casinos and doing some local sight-seeing, but the passion of Vegas surrounded them and they decided to end their mini-vacation by saying "I do" with a twist!

Following seven simple steps, here is how John and Christina planned their unique wedding in less than 24 hours:

Step 1. Discuss your wedding wishes.

John always wanted the big, traditional wedding, while Christina was not interested in a grand gala. The couple met in college, had been dating for five years, and had lived together for the previous three years. Everyone expected that a marriage proposal was imminent, but the idea of planning a traditional wedding was daunting to both of them. "We both have very large families and we knew that we would have to save money for three or fours years just to pay for the wedding," said John. "We really didn't like the idea of putting our wedding off for so long. For us, the marriage was more important than the wedding."

These initial conversations about the pros and cons of planning a traditional wedding helped to plant the seed for the couple to consider a unique wedding. Still, John and Christina had not yet announced a formal engagement and were not certain of the type of wedding they would ultimately choose.

Step 2. Consider an elopement.

On the second-to-last day of John's convention and Christina's visit to Las Vegas, the couple was enjoying the excitement of the city. "All of a sudden," recalls Christina, "John got this look in his eye that I had never seen before and said 'Let's get married!'" John was serious about his proposal and the idea of an elopement had always appealed to Christina, so the couple spent that Sunday afternoon shopping for an engagement ring and wedding bands, the couple's most significant wedding details.

Step 3. Research the legal requirements.

After five hours of ring shopping, the couple returned to their hotel and asked the concierge how to go about getting a marriage license in Las Vegas. The concierge directed the couple to the Marriage License Bureau at the Clark County Courthouse, which is open until midnight, seven days a week. This worked out well for John and Christina, who already had tickets to a show that they didn't want to miss. They strolled into the courthouse just before midnight on Sunday evening, were deemed by the clerk to be of "sound mind," paid the $55 license fee, and received one of more than 600 marriage licenses issued that day!

Step 4. Choose a wedding location.

After obtaining their marriage license, John and Christina returned to their hotel with the intent to marry the following day. When they awoke on Monday morning, they decided to call the New York-New York Hotel and Casino to see if they could get married there, given that one of their first trips together as a couple was to New York City. When they spoke to the hotel's wedding coordinator, the person was surprised to hear that the couple wanted to get married *that day*. The coordinator told the couple that the hotel did not accommodate last-minute weddings and that they would need to prebook their wedding.

Prebook a wedding in Las Vegas? Wasn't this the mecca of last-minute weddings? The couple called around to several other major hotels, including the MGM Grand, the Venetian, and the Paris Hilton and were not only shocked that none of these hotels could accommodate a same-day wedding, but that all of the hotel wedding coordinators were surprised that the couple was inquiring about such a wedding!

John and Christina learned that it is not as easy as the guidebooks tell you to get married in Las Vegas. Sure, they could have traveled to the outskirts of town to participate in a drive-through Elvis wedding, but they wanted something a bit more sophisticated.

At 10 on Monday morning, the wedding coordinator at the Monte Carlo, the hotel at which John and Christina were staying, arrived and was able to help the couple to plan a same-day wedding.

Step 5. Finalize wedding day details.

Still surprised at the couple's last-minute request, the wedding coordinator at the Monte Carlo masterfully orchestrated a wedding ceremony in under two hours. While John and Christina relaxed in their hotel room, the coordinator reserved the hotel chapel, called a minister, recruited a photographer, ordered a wedding bouquet and boutonnière, and chilled champagne in time for a noon wedding.

Step 6. Exchange your vows.

After meeting individually for several minutes with the minister, the couple, dressed in their casual vacation clothes, exchanged vows in a simple ceremony witnessed by the photographer and the hotel wedding coordinators.

Step 7. Enjoy the wedding "reception."

Not the gambling types, John and Christina doubted they would return to Las Vegas anytime soon, so they spent the afternoon of their wedding day sight-seeing in Nevada and caught a late-evening plane back home.

Dealing With the Elopement Aftermath

When they returned home from Las Vegas, John and Christina announced the news of their wedding to family and friends. The reactions were mixed. Christina's family was thrilled with the news, but John's family was less enthusiastic. "I come from a large, Italian Catholic family. When I told my parents that Christina and I got married, my mom responded in disbelief saying, 'You're joking, right?' She really wanted the large traditional wedding, as did one of my sisters who is very tied to the Catholic faith. They kept asking us when our 'real' wedding would be. Eventually, they got over it and were very happy for us."

The couple's friends also took the news differently. "Most of our friends loved it, but my best friend was disappointed that I didn't call him to fly out for the wedding," said John. "We are not very spontaneous people at all—we usually over-think everything—and my friend is very spontaneous and would have liked to have been there. I also think he was disappointed that he couldn't give me a Bachelor party and be a part of the celebration. He felt left out initially, but he got over it too."

Tips For Other Eloping Couples

1. Plan in advance. As John and Christina realized, it may not be as easy to get married in Las Vegas as you think. If you want something other than a drive-through wedding, at least call the hotel ahead of time to check on chapel availability.

2. But don't plan too much! "If we had planned our wedding, I don't think it would have happened because so many people would have tried to talk us out of it," said Christina. In fact, one of her colleagues was so excited about John and Christina's Las Vegas wedding that he and his

fiancée started planning a destination wedding to Vegas. The guest list began to get out of hand, however, and they ended up sacrificing their Las Vegas wedding for a traditional one.

3. Make sure that you both want to elope. John and Christina had discussed their wedding wishes ahead of time and knew that getting married was more important to them than having a wedding. Making certain that both the bride and the groom are eager to elope will avoid regrets.

$ *Christina and John's Las Vegas Elopement Details* $

Hotel wedding package (including chapel, flowers, champagne, and photo album)	= $375
Officiant	= $100
Photographer and 30 negatives	= $200
Marriage license fee	= $55
Marriage certificate	= $10
Total elopement costs	= $740*
Total planning time	=24 hours

   * Because John and Christina got married while on a business convention, John's company paid for the flights and hotel.

Las Vegas Wedding Resources

> - Clark County Marriage License Information. *http://www.co.clark.nv.us/clerk/ Marriage_Information.htm*
> - Las Vegas Chamber of Commerce. *www.lvchamber.com/*
> - Las Vegas Convention and Visitors Authority (includes information on local chapels and bridal shops). *www.lasvegas24hours.com/*
> - Las Vegas Helicopters—Combine an elopement and adventure wedding by getting married over the skies of Las Vegas! *www.lvhelicopters.com/*
> - Monte Carlo Resort and Casino. *www.monte-carlo.com*
> - Aladdin Resort and Casino. *www.aladdincasino.com/*
> - Caesar's Palace. *www.caesars.com/Caesars/ LasVegas*
> - Circus Circus Resort and Casino—Combine an elopement and theme wedding by getting married at Circus Circus, complete with a five-acre amusement park! *www.circuscircus.com*

Elopement Venues

Elopements are gaining in popularity! The following lists wedding venues by U.S. state (plus Canada) that cater to elopers:

Alabama

Lodge on Gorham's Bluff—A private country inn overlooking the Tennessee River Valley, the Lodge offers breathtaking views for intimate wedding ceremonies and features a personalized, on-site wedding planner. *www.gorhamsbluff.com*

Alaska

Holland America Cruise Lines—Get married atop an Alaskan glacier or aboard your cruise ship with Holland America's Alaskan cruises. Elopement packages, which include ceremony, wedding coordinator, flowers, cake, and champagne start at $1,295. *www.hollandamerica.com*

Arizona

Apple Orchard Inn—Offering an elopement package beginning at $550 plus accommodations, this bed-and-breakfast offers an ideal backdrop for a private wedding. *www.appleorchardbb.com*

Arkansas

Angel at Rose Hall—Nestled in Eureka Springs, this bed-and-breakfast offers an elopement package, priced at just $150. *www.eurekaspringsangel.com*

Lookout Point Lakeside Inn Bed and Breakfast—A lakefront inn in Hot Springs, this bed and breakfast offers several romantic elopement packages, starting at $135. *www.lookoutpointinn.com*

Ridgeway House—Also located in Eureka Springs, this historic bed-and-breakfast specializes in elopements. Packages begin at $550. *www.ridgewayhouse.com*

Rock Cottage Gardens—A quaint bed-and-breakfast with on-site chapel, its deluxe elopement package is priced at just over $350, including ceremony and 2-nights' accommodations. *www.rockcottagegardens.com*

The Empress of Little Rock—This historic inn offers a special elopement package, including ceremony and two nights' accommodations, for $750. *www.theempress.com*

California

Blue Violet Mansion Bed and Breakfast—If eloping to a mansion in Napa is more to your liking, then consider the Blue Violet Mansion Bed and Breakfast. The mansion supports elopements and packages start at $1,000. *www.bluevioletmansion.com*

Casa Laguna Inn—If an elopement retreat to Laguna Beach sounds exciting, check out this elegant oceanfront bed-and-breakfast that offers elopement packages beginning at $750. *www.casalaguna.com*

Forest Suites Resort—Nestled in Lake Tahoe, this intimate resort with on-site wedding chapel offers all-inclusive elopement packages beginning at $700. *www.forestsuites.com*

Heritage House Inn—Located in Mendocino, this oceanfront inn offers an all-inclusive elopement package for $1,000. *www.heritagehouseinn.com*

La Belle Époque—Given as a wedding gift in 1893 from a father to his daughter, who was married in the parlor of this luxurious inn, this downtown Napa bed-and-breakfast offers an intimate elopement package for $500, plus accommodations. *www.labelleepoque.com*

Colorado

Romantic Riversong Inn—Elope while snowshoeing through a National Park or while walking through a sunlit meadow. Riversong caters to elopers and offers a complete elopement package starting at $475, plus accommodations at the bed-and-breakfast. *www.mycoloradowedding.com*

Stanley Hotel—A majestic hotel in Estes Park, elopement packages including ceremony details, meals and accommodations, begin at $1,000. *www.stanleyhotel.com*

Taharaa Mountain Lodge—For a unique elopement wedding in the heart of the Rocky Mountains, consider this luxury bed-and-breakfast resort. Elopement packages start at $385, plus accommodations. *www.taharaa.com*

Wyman Hotel and Inn—Located in Silverton, this inn in an old mining town offers several comprehensive elopement packages, starting at $645. *www.thewyman.com*

Connecticut

A Cardinal House—A bed-and-breakfast located in Glastonbury, this inn's primary business is small weddings and elopements. The basic elopement package is priced at $220, while the deluxe package, including meals and accommodations, is priced at $695. *www.acardinalhouse.com*

Angels' Watch Inn—A romantic bed-and-breakfast located along the Connecticut Valley shoreline, this inn offers a generous elopement package that includes two-nights' accommodations, justice of the peace, witness, flowers and cake, photography and video, champagne toast, keepsake flutes and cheese, and transportation to and reservations at a nearby restaurant. The elopement package is priced at $695. *www.angelswatchinn.com*

Deacon Timothy Pratt Bed and Breakfast—A quaint, New England bed-and-breakfast located in Old Saybrook, this inn offers an inclusive elopement package starting at $350. *www.pratthouse.net*

Delaware

Sea Witch Manor Inn and Spa—This romantic, adults-only retreat located on Rehoboth Beach offers indulgent amenities and small wedding services. *www.seawitchmanor.com*

Florida

Casa Morada—A luxurious, 16-suite hotel in the Florida Keys, Casa Morada's deluxe, all-inclusive Sunset Elopement Package is priced just under $2,000. *www.casamorada.com*

Center Court Historic Inn and Cottages—Located in beautiful Key West, the innkeeper of this bed-and-breakfast inn specializes in performing unique elopement ceremonies, with packages starting at $75. *www.centercourtkw.com*

Georgia

Beach Bed and Breakfast—A luxurious bed-and-breakfast overlooking the Atlantic Ocean, this inn caters to elopement ceremonies. *www.beachbedandbreakfast.com*

Hawaii

Hilton Waikoloa Village—Located on the "Big Island" of Hawaii, this full-service resort with its own wedding chapel offers "a la carte" elopement packages as well as complete packages starting at $1,100. *www.hiltonwaikoloavillage.com*

Kauai Marriott Resort and Beach Club—A deluxe resort located on Kalapaki Beach on one of Hawaii's most romantic islands, the Kauai Marriott provides exceptional service for eloping couples. Elopement packages begin at $1,000. *www.marriotthawaii.com/kauai.html*

Sheraton Waikiki—Located in the heart of Honolulu, this full-service resort offers several elopement packages beginning at $1,000. *www.sheratonwaikiki.com*

Westin Maui—Located on Kaanapali Beach, this resort offers several elopement packages. Deluxe packages start at $1,350, or you can create your own "a la carte" elopement. *www.westinmaui.com*

Idaho

Blue Heron Inn—Located on the banks of the Snake River, this romantic bed-and-breakfast accommodates small weddings, with inclusive packages starting at $450. *www.idahoblueheron.com*

Illinois

Beall Mansion—An elegant bed and breakfast located in Alton, this inn offers an elopement package starting at $600, with one night's accommodations. *www.beallmansion.com*

Pinehill Inn—Located in Oregon, Illinois, this luxurious inn caters to small weddings and planned elopements, with rates starting at $80/hour. *www.pinehillbb.com*

Indiana

Old Bridge Inn Bed and Breakfast—A quaint country inn located on the Indiana/Kentucky border, this bed-and-breakfast accommodates old-fashioned parlor weddings. Room rates begin at $65/night. *www.oldbridgeinn.com*

Iowa

The Wedding Chapel—A wedding chapel in West De Moines, this location focuses on intimate ceremonies and elopements. The elopement packages, which include chapel, non-denominational minister, silk flowers, and music, start at $295. *www.dmweddingchapel.com*

Kansas

Pickering House—This inn located in Olathe provides elopement services, including outdoor weddings in a private gazebo or indoor ceremonies in a formal Victorian parlor. The hosts can assist with all wedding preparations, including selecting the officiant, florist, cake, food, and entertainment. *www.pickeringhouse.com*

Kentucky

1851 Historic Maple Hill Manor—A 600-acre Greek revival plantation home, this bed-and-breakfast inn was purchased as a wedding gift by Thomas McElroy to his bride. Today, it offers romantic elopement packages for couples that are free with overnight accommodations. *www.maplehillmanor.com*

Louisiana

Les Carillons—A historic bed-and-breakfast located in New Orleans, this inn offers elopement packages beginning at $250. *www.artsbb.com*

Magnolia Mansion—If a New Orleans-style elopement in an historic mansion sounds appealing, consider Magnolia Mansion. Elopement packages, which include ceremony, photos, champagne, cake, and one night's accommodations, start at $800. *www.magnoliamansion.com*

Wyndham Bourbon Orleans—A historic hotel located in the heart of the French Quarter, the hotel function coordinators can accommodate intimate weddings and elopements. *www.wyndham.com*

Maine

Lakehouse Bed and Breakfast—A country inn located in Westford in the foothills of the White Mountains, this inn specializes in elopements and offers a generous package for $800, including two nights' accommodations. *www.lakehousemaine.com*

Maryland

Elk Forge Bed and Breakfast—Located in Elkton, this historic inn and day spa offers an inclusive "Magical Moments Elopement Package" starting at $589. *www.elkforge.com*

Massachusetts

Carriage House Inn—Located on beautiful Cape Cod, this romantic bed-and-breakfast offers all-inclusive elopement packages starting at $500. *www.thecarriagehouseinn.com*

Thorncroft Inn—A first-class inn located on the romantic island of Martha's Vineyard, this inn focuses exclusively on preparing intimate elopements. The inn can arrange all wedding details for free with a confirmed room reservation. *www.thorncroft.com*

Michigan

The Listening Inn—For a remote, rustic elopement in the Michigan wilderness, check out the renovated Listening Inn. *www.thelisteninginn.com*

The Seymour House—Located in South Haven, this bed and breakfast is a romantic haven for elopers. The inn offers generous elopement packages, starting at $565. *www.seymourhouse.com*

Minnesota

Thayer's Historic Bed and Breakfast—Located in Annandale, this quaint country inn offers a "We Want Simple" wedding package for two. This all-inclusive package is priced at $300. *www.thayers.net*

Mississippi

1902-08 Stained Glass Manor—Located in Vicksburg, this quaint bed-and-breakfast offers small wedding and elopement packages beginning at $250. *www.vickbnb.com*

Camille House Bed and Breakfast—Located in Gulfport on the Gulf of Mexico, this small bed-and-breakfast accommodates intimate weddings and elopements. *www.camillehouse.com*

Missouri

Emory Creek Bed and Breakfast—A Victorian inn located in Branson, the innkeepers accommodate intimate weddings and elopements Sunday through Thursday and provide all wedding arrangements. Elopement packages start at $300, including ceremony and accommodations. *www.emorycreekbnb.com*

Loganberry Inn—Located halfway between Kansas City and St. Louis, this delightful bed-and-breakfast hosts intimate weddings and elopements. The basic elopement package is priced at $325. *www.loganberryinn.com*

Montana

320 Guest Ranch and Resort—For an authentic Blue Sky ranch elopement, consider the 320 Guest Ranch and Resort. They have hosted many weddings for two and will customize an elopement package to fit your needs. *www.320ranch.com*

Nebraska

Cornerstone Mansion—Located in Omaha's historic Gold Coast, this bed-and-breakfast caters to small weddings. *www.cornerstonemansion.com*

Nevada

Little Chapel of the Flowers—Performs more than 7,000 elopements and destination weddings each year. Elopement packages start at under $200. *www.littlechapel.com*

New Hampshire

Hideaway Inn—Located in New London, this country inn offers a variety of elopement packages, starting at $250. *www.hideawayinn.com*

Notchland Inn—A charming country inn in the heart of the White Mountains, this inn provides elopement packages starting at $975, including ceremony, all wedding details, meals, and accommodations. *www.notchland.com*

Rosewood Country Inn—Located in the lovely Mount Sunapee Lake region, this romantic bed-and-breakfast offers a comprehensive elopement package for $350, plus accommodations. *www.rosewoodcountryinn.com*

New Jersey

La Maison Inn—An elegant French country inn located in Spring Lake, this bed and breakfast accommodates intimate weddings and elopements. *www.lamaisoninn.com*

New Mexico

Hacienda de Colores—Located in Albuquerque, this Spanish-style bed-and-breakfast features an elopement package priced at $375, which includes an officiant and honeymoon suite. *www.haciendadecolores.com*

Hacienda Vargas Bed and Breakfast and Wedding Chapel—Plan your elopement at a Rio Grande Valley inn that focuses on small weddings and elopements. Inclusive elopement packages begin at $450. *www.haciendavargas.com*

New York

Central Park—While you have to submit a wedding application and pay an application fee of $300 to get married in the romantic Conservatory Garden, an elopement wedding in Central Park is a magical event. To get married in other sections of the park, the permit fee is $25. *www.centralparknyc.org*

North Carolina

Old Stone Inn and Restaurant—Located in Waynesville, this rustic bed-and-breakfast accommodates small weddings and elopements. Elopement packages start at $925, including three nights' accommodations, ceremony, flowers, cake, and a gourmet wedding dinner for two. *www.oldstoneinn.com*

North Dakota

Old School Bed and Breakfast—Located in the small town of Arnegard, the innkeeper of this quaint bed-and-breakfast can arrange small religious or civil elopement ceremonies with accommodations at the inn. *www.oldschoolbb.com*

Ohio

A Georgian Manner—Elope in casual elegance overlooking Lake Logan. This romantic bed-and-breakfast offers elopement packages beginning at $300. *www.georgianmanner.com*

Whispering Pines Bed and Breakfast—Overlooking Atwood Lake, this romantic inn offers an elopement package starting at $275. *www.atwoodlake.com*

Oklahoma

Red Stone Country Inn and Wedding Chapels—Located in Guthrie, this unique wedding chapel and bed-and-breakfast venue provide a romantic spot for an elopement. Packages begin at $250. *www.redstonebb.com*

Oregon

Overleaf Lodge—Located on the Oregon coast in Yachats, this resort features privacy and romance that will make your elopement wedding sparkle. The resort wedding coordinators can help you plan an intimate wedding by referring you to local wedding vendors. *www.overleaflodge.com*

Pennsylvania

Hillside Farm Bed and Breakfast—For an elopement get-away amidst the Amish fields of Lancaster County Pennsylvania, check out Hillside Farm Bed and Breakfast. The inn offers a special elopement package for $630 which includes accommodations breakfast for two nights, a ceremony performed by the town mayor, and cake and champagne. *www.hillsidefarmbandb.com*

Rhode Island

Atlantic Inn—Off the Rhode Island coast on the lovely Block Island, the Atlantic Inn caters to small, personalized weddings. *www.atlanticinn.com*

South Carolina

The Cypress Inn—Perched on the banks of the Waccamaw River in Conway, this bed and breakfast focuses exclusively on elopements and intimate weddings. Their elopement package is priced at $800 and includes officiant, flowers, photography, and two nights' accommodations at the inn. *www.acypressinn.com*

South Dakota

Triangle Ranch—A rustic ranch located near the Badlands National Park, Triangle Ranch provides a generous "Just for Two" all-inclusive wedding package priced at $400. *www.bbonline.com/sd/triangleranch*

Tennessee

Christopher Place Resort—Rated one of the top 10 romantic inns in America, this elegant resort in Newport offers an "Affair for Two" deluxe elopement package starting at $899. *www.christopherplace.com*

Iron Mountain Inn—A beautiful bed-and-breakfast tucked in the Tennessee hills, this inn specializes in elopements. It offers a personalized elopement package for $575, including ceremony and accommodations. *www.ironmountaininn.com*

Timber Rose English Lodge—Abutting Great Smoky Mountains National Park, this elegant inn offers elopement packages beginning at $250. *www.timberrose.com*

Top 'O Woodland Bed and Breakfast—A historic inn located in Nashville, this bed-and-breakfast offers its own wedding chapel and will perform elopements starting at $150. *www.topofwoodland.com*

Texas

Hidden Oaks Bed and Breakfast—Located in Houston, this charming country inn specializes in boutique weddings and elopements. Special elopement packages are priced at $550 and include ceremony and accommodations. *www.hiddenoaksbnb.com*

Inn at Craig Place—Located in San Antonio, this romantic bed-and-breakfast specializes in intimate weddings and elopements, starting at $285. *www.craigplace.com*

Utah

Angel House Inn Bed and Breakfast—Located in Park City, this romantic inn accommodates small weddings and all-inclusive elopements. *www.angelhouseinn.com*

Vermont

Arlington Inn—Located in Southern Vermont, this country bed and breakfast offers a deluxe elopement package starting at $985. *www.arlingtoninn.com*

Grey Gables Mansion—A historic bed-and-breakfast located in Richford, the innkeepers offer a special all-inclusive elopement package for $525. *www.greygablesmansion.com*

Hartness House—A historic inn located in Springfield, the Hartness House offers a comprehensive Vermont Elope Package priced at $695, including ceremony, meals, and accommodations. *www.hartnesshouse.com*

White Rocks Inn—Enjoy an elopement retreat at a quintessential New England country inn. Elopement packages, which include accommodations, ceremony, photography, flowers and a wedding cake, begin at $500. *www.whiterocksinn.com*

Virginia

White Fence Bed and Breakfast—Starting at under $600, this Shenandoah Valley inn's elopement packages include ceremony, meals, and accommodations. *www.whitefencebb.com*

Williamsburg Manor Bed and Breakfast—For an elegant elopement in the heart of colonial Williamsburg, consider visiting the Williamsburg Manor Bed and Breakfast. The innkeepers were married at the Manor in 1996 and cater to small weddings and elopements. An all-inclusive package consists of ceremony and officiant, flowers, cake and champagne, nearby dinner reservations, music, photography and one night's accommodations at the inn. This package is priced at $675. *www.williamsburg-manor.com*

Washington

The Resort at Deer Harbor—A luxurious resort on a waterfront location, this hotel offers an elopement package (available October to June) that includes deluxe accommodations and ceremony for $1,000. *www.deerharbor.com*

Turtleback Farm Inn and Orchard House—A traditional country inn located in the heart of the San Juan Islands, this retreat focuses exclusively on elopement weddings. The deluxe package, including ceremony, photography, flowers, cake, and champagne, is priced at $1,000. *www.turtlebackinn.com*

Warm Springs Inn—Located on the lovely Wenatchee River, this romantic bed-and-breakfast offers a full-service elopement package including ceremony, lodging, and dinner for approximately $500. *www.warmspringsinn.com*

West Virginia

Country Chalet Bed and Breakfast—Located in southern West Virginia, this casual, rustic inn offers a small wedding package. *www.countrychalet.com*

Wisconsin

Lazy Cloud Lodge—A romantic getaway in Lake Geneva, this bed-and-breakfast takes the hassle out of wedding planning by creating a perfect elopement wedding for you. Elopement packages start at $225 plus accommodations. *www.lazycloud.com*

White Rose Bed and Breakfast—For an elegant elopement with all the details attended to by your innkeepers, consider this Wisconsin Dells bed-and-breakfast. Elopement ceremony packages begin at $300. *www.thewhiterose.com*

Wyoming

Nagle Warren Mansion—Located in Cheyenne, this historic bed-and-breakfast offers a romantic, all-inclusive elopement package. *www.naglewarrenmansion.com*

Canada

A Bear and Bison Inn—A charming country inn in Alberta, this bed-and-breakfast offers several generous elopement packages, beginning at $1,100. *www.bearandbisoninn.com*

Castlebury Cottage—Elope to an enchanted castle in the Vancouver Islands! Castlebury Cottage caters to elopers and offers an array of elopement options. *www.castleburycottage.com*

Hummingbird Hill Bed, Breakfast and Spa—This romantic bed-and-breakfast located in Astorville, Ontario, offers customized, all-inclusive elopement packages beginning at $1,350. *www.hummingbirdhill.ca*

Marriott Fallsview—Imagine getting married in a chapel 23 stories above Niagara Falls! This luxurious resort offers several wedding packages, including a simple wedding package for two starting at $750. *www.niagarafallsmarriott.com*

Elopement Resources

Hagen, Shelly. *The Everything Elopement Book: Avoid the Wedding Chaos!* Adams Media, 2004.

Shaw, Scott and Lynn Beahan. *Let's Elope! The Definitive Guide to Eloping, Destination Weddings, and Other Creative Wedding Options.* Bantam, 2001.

Tabb, Lisa and Sam Silverstein. *Beyond Vegas: 25 Exotic Wedding and Elopement Destinations Around the World.* McGraw-Hill, 2000

Warner, Diane. *Picture-Perfect, Worry Free Weddings: 72 Destinations and Venues.* Betterway, 1998.

Chapter 6

Destination Weddings

If the idea of a private elopement is too lonely and impersonal for you, then join the thousands of couples who plan destination weddings with friends and loved ones. Sometimes called "weddingmoons," destination weddings are typically small gatherings of close family members and friends who fly with you to a distant place to enjoy a wedding away. The most popular of today's non-traditional weddings, destination weddings have many advantages for couples seeking a unique and memorable wedding day surrounded by special guests.

You may want to plan a destination wedding if:

> You like the idea of an elopement but want something a bit more inclusive.

> You want to be surrounded by close family members and friends.

> You are flexible and don't need to be in control of every wedding detail.

> You like to travel.

> Your loved ones would need to travel for your wedding anyway.

> You like the idea of a neutral wedding location.

139

> You want your guests to have a good time.
> You want to save money.
> You don't mind dealing with long-distance wedding vendors.
> You want to plan a unique wedding celebration that will be memorable for you and your guests.
> You want to combine an intimate ceremony with a post-wedding party.

Avoid Logistical Strife

One benefit to planning a destination wedding is that it can help you to avoid disagreements with loved ones about where your wedding celebration should be held. If you are like many of today's engaged couples, you are much more mobile than your parents were a generation ago and you likely live away from your childhood home. You also may have friends and other family members who are scattered around the world. As you plan your wedding, you may be discovering that travel costs will be a burden for many of your guests and will add to wedding costs and hassles.

Disgruntlement may also be smoldering when one set of parents expects the wedding to be held in their hometown, while the other parents want to see you tie the knot nearer to them. Sound familiar? Torn couples like you often choose a destination wedding where they invite guests to travel to a fun or exotic location to enjoy a combined wedding and vacation and avoid logistical conflicts.

It is important to note, however, that many family members and friends might find it just as inconvenient, and perhaps more costly, to attend a destination wedding. No matter which destination you choose, you will likely be showered with opinions about your chosen destination and urged to make changes. To avoid mounting conflict, take the advice of other destination wedding couples, including those featured in this chapter, and stay committed to your wedding destination. Be aware, however, that, if you are choosing a destination wedding, your guests are not obligated to attend and many may find the travel expectation too much of a burden. If you have dreams of all of your loved ones and friends surrounding you on your wedding day, then a destination wedding may not be the best choice for you because some guests likely will not attend. Give heartfelt invitations to the people you truly hope will attend your destination wedding, but be prepared to go it alone if guests do not want to travel with you.

Easy Planning

Another benefit of a destination wedding is that it can be planned in a relatively short time and take very little effort. The number of couples choosing a destination wedding has quadrupled over the past decade and many resort destinations have taken notice. Nearly every popular vacation spot has resources for couples planning a wedding away, and most offer significant discounts on hotel rates, rental cars, and guest activities. Even airlines have joined in. Major airlines such as American and US Airways offer group airfare discounts for wedding parties of more than 10 people.

While it definitely does not require the average 250 hours of planning associated with a traditional wedding, a destination wedding does require some forethought and organization. You will need to investigate destination wedding marriage requirements. You will want to book hotels, wedding services, and airfare several months prior to your wedding to ensure availability and take advantage of advanced booking discounts. You will also want to give your

guests as much time as possible to plan their vacation schedules and budgets. As a courtesy to your guests—and to im-
prove your yield—try to send out "Save the Date" notices
at least six months in advance for smaller destination weddings, and up to a year in advance for larger wedding parties. With your "Save the Date" notices, you may also think
about sending Website links or an informational booklet on
your travel destination to get guests excited about the trip.
Many wedding Websites also allow you to create your own
free Website to post information about your wedding, travel
itineraries, hotel information, recreation ideas, special mes-
sages, and more. Check out *www.weddingchannel.com* to create a personalized destination wedding Website for your guests.

In addition to making your own reservations, sending out
"Save the Date" notices, creating a week-long guest itinerary,
and finalizing wedding day details, planning a destination wedding also requires you to check in on your guests' planning
frequently to make certain that they are as organized as you
are! While most destination wedding couples suggest that you
have your guests make their own travel arrangements, it is a
good idea to check in with your guests periodically to make
sure that their planning is going smoothly and that all of their
questions and concerns have been addressed.

Fun for the Whole Family

Free from wedding tradition and typical planning challenges, destination weddings are enjoyable for the bride and
groom and their guests. Make sure you build into your destination wedding itinerary plenty of time for your guests to enjoy themselves and explore their surroundings, without your
wedding being the primary focus. Planning a destination wedding is really about spending some down time with the people
you care about the most. Your wedding day should be second-
ary. If you want to be the center of attention and have your
destination wedding experience focused entirely on you, then
opt for another wedding format.

The intimate nature of destination weddings often can cause discontentment among your loved ones. Family members and friends who are not invited to your wedding may feel hurt and unvalued. The guest selection process is often long and arduous, and likely the most challenging part of planning a destination wedding. In fact, many couples who initially select a destination wedding ultimately abandon the idea when guest lists spin out of control. Some of these couples choose another type of non-traditional wedding, such as an elopement or surprise wedding, while other couples give in to a traditional wedding.

Manage the Guest List

Although finalizing the guest list can be a major hurdle in your destination wedding planning, it need not jeopardize your plans. Here are three helpful hints for finalizing your guest list for your destination wedding:

1. Explore your options. Before announcing your destination wedding to your loved ones, you and your partner should decide on a budget and talk with your hotel wedding coordinator or destination wedding planner about availability and pricing options. You may find from this process that certain destinations can offer plenty more options when the guest list is 15 people compared to 30, for example. You may also discover an optimal guest number that will allow you to pamper your guests while staying within your budget.

2. Rank your guests. After you and your partner decide on a location, arrange initial contracts with your hotel function coordinator or wedding planner, and decide on an optimal number of guests, start selecting the people to invite to your wedding. Each of you should create a list of the people you would like to attend, with a rating system for each person. While it sounds impersonal, rating your guests on a scale of 1 to 3, for example, will help you to prioritize your guest list. Using this scale, identify the people whom you could not bear being without (1); the people whom you would really like to attend but who are not critical (2); and the people whom you would enjoy having but could eliminate if necessary (3).

3. Defend your calculations. Once you and your partner narrow down your guest list in accordance with your budget and destination wedding expectations, then spread the word. If you receive criticisms from loved ones regarding your guest list (and you will!), then simply explain that you and your partner went through a deliberate and calculated planning process to ensure an optimal number of guests for your wedding. Of course, as with all wedding planning—traditional or not—if other people will be paying for your wedding, your bargaining power may be more limited. In this case, try to stay committed to your wedding plans but be willing to compromise—either by inviting fewer guests and paying for your own wedding or inviting additional guests not included on your original list.

Destination Wedding Trade-Offs

Pros	Cons
They can be inexpensive compared to traditional weddings.	The guest list can spin out of control.
They involve family members and friends.	They may be expensive or inconvenient for guests.
They are great if guests would need to travel to your wedding anyhow.	Family members and friends may dissuade you from planning a wedding away.
They can take little planning time and effort.	They can require a lot of organization and follow-up.
They can be fun for everyone.	They can be disappointing if some guests are not able to attend. (cont'd)

They avoid planning strife and stress.	They can be stressful if you are responsible for guest reservations and logistics.
They can occur in beautiful spots around the world.	Many family members and friends may feel left out and hurt.

Destination Wedding Checklist

Now that you have grappled with some of the benefits and drawbacks of a destination wedding, and are committed to giving it a try, it is time to start planning. While the Step-by-Step Non-Traditional Wedding Planner in Chapter 4 can give you in-depth information on planning your unique wedding, here are few planning tips specific to weddingmooners:

6 Months to 1 Year Prior

Plan Your Budget

While destination weddings can be significantly cheaper than traditional weddings and you can get a lot more for your money, costs can quickly skyrocket. Decide how much you and your partner want to spend on your destination wedding and then begin to investigate your options. It is generally customary for the bride and groom to pay for attendants' lodging, but you are not required to. Just don't be disappointed if some members of your bridal party are unable to attend due to the cost. Guests will typically pay for their own travel and lodging expenses, though if you have money in your budget to treat your guests, it is a wonderful touch that will be greatly appreciated.

Deciding on a budget before your formal planning begins can also help you in the vendor negotiation process. For example, if you tell your hotel wedding coordinator that you are only looking to spend $100 for your flowers, then you will be able to ask her what she can provide within that price range as opposed to letting her sell you on a higher-priced package. Consider using the Non-Traditional Wedding Budget Planner in Chapter 4 to help you with this important planning step.

You will also want to be aware of current exchange rates in various destination spots to see how much you can get for your money. For many locations, you can purchase a dream wedding for far less than it would cost in U.S. dollars. For up-to-the-minute international currency conversions, check out the Yahoo! Finance Website at: *http://finance.yahoo.com/m3?u.*

Select a Destination

Once you agree on a wedding budget, start looking at your favorite travel spots for information on marriage requirements and availability of wedding planning resources. For a destination wedding, it is a good idea to use a hotel function coordinator or local wedding planner to help you with your efforts. This will save you a lot of time, money, and aggravation and will provide some peace of mind that your wedding vendors are trustworthy and reliable. Also, the marriage requirements for many popular wedding destinations can be complicated and a wedding coordinator can help you navigate this process.

When selecting a destination, think about the style of destination wedding that interests you. Will your wedding be large and formal? Or will your wedding be small and casual? Do you want to incorporate local customs or do you have specific expectations for your wedding day?

Choose a wedding style that is right for you and that will be engaging for your guests. It is important to realize, however, that if you have a picture-perfect image of your wedding in your mind, then you should think twice about planning a destination wedding. This unique wedding option requires you to give up significant control of your wedding planning and rely on distant vendors to coordinate your nuptials. Destination weddings are most successful when you allow local flare to shine through—in flowers, entertainment, and ceremonial customs. Let go and trust your wedding planners to create an authentic destination wedding experience for you and your loved ones.

As you decide on a destination, you may also want to choose a location that is safe and welcoming to foreigners. Given the precarious state of world affairs, many locations may not be hospitable to visitors, particularly Westerners. Check out the U.S. Department of State's Website for a list of current travel advisories: *http://travel.state.gov/*.

Finally, when selecting your destination and wedding date, keep in mind the various seasons of your travel spot. Guests may not be excited to travel to the Caribbean during hurricane season, for example; nor would you want to deal with the uncertainty of the tropics during their rainy season.

Finalize Your Guest List

As mentioned earlier, finalizing your guest list will likely be your most difficult planning step. Sit down as a couple to select your wedding day witnesses. You might also choose to invite more people to your destination wedding than you expect to attend, just to be inclusive. This is a nice gesture, but be prepared for the possibility that all guests may attend.

Send "Save the Date" Notices

Give your guests plenty of notice about your destination wedding plans to help them arrange their vacation schedules and make necessary travel arrangements. Your "Save the Date" notices can be formal announcements or simple e-mails. With the "Save the Date" notice, be sure to include information about the date, time, and location of your wedding, as well as local hotels and rates, any travel discounts that you have identified, and local resources for visitors. If your destination wedding will be overseas, include information on passport requirements, currency conversions, and cultural norms.

4 to 6 Months Prior

Finalize Wedding Contracts

The old saying "the devil is in the details" is particularly true for destination weddings. Because your wedding will be held far away, you will want to finalize all contracts and wedding details at least four months prior to your wedding day. Make sure that you get all wedding plans in writing. If you expect the florist to bring your flowers at a certain time, make sure it is in writing. If you want your photographer to take action shots as opposed to posed portraits, make sure it is in writing. When planning a destination wedding, remember to be a P.E.S.T.—Persistent, Explicit, Straightforward, Timely.

Decide on Wedding Attire

If you will be purchasing wedding attire prior to your wedding trip, now is the time to start looking. If you will have bridesmaids or groomsmen joining you for your ceremony, decide on their wedding attire. Many destination wedding couples choose to marry in clothes that reflect the unique culture or traditions of the wedding location. If this interests you, begin now to research options and availability. This would be a good opportunity to use your hotel wedding coordinator or local wedding planner for assistance.

As you finalize your travel arrangements at this time, you may also want to check with your airline or local shipping company regarding sending your wedding attire and other wedding supplies to your destination.

2 to 4 Months Prior

Plan a Post-Wedding Celebration

Many destination wedding couples decide that while they want their ceremony to be an intimate affair witnessed by a few close loved ones, they want to host a party with their remaining family members and friends upon their return. If this option interests you, then begin to plan your post-wedding celebration several months prior to your wedding day. This post-wedding celebration (it is usually not called a reception) can be formal or informal. Just be aware that many loved ones may guide you toward planning a traditional wedding reception that can cause expenses to mount and tempers to flare.

Of course, some couples choose to compromise on the post-wedding celebration in order to plan their destination wedding. If loved ones are outraged by a non-traditional wedding—and will be footing the bill—you may be able to ease tensions by suggesting a non-traditional ceremony in a far-off location followed by a formal celebration back home. If you decide to host a post-wedding party—whether modest or grand—now is the time to start your planning and reserving.

Create Your Guest Itinerary

A destination wedding is a lively and engaging experience—and a vacation—for your guests. Help your guests make the most of the occasion by creating a list of possible activities that they can enjoy during your wedding week. Be careful not to make any events mandatory and not to structure your guests' time too strictly. Provide them with suggestions and guidelines and then leave them alone to enjoy their vacation as they choose.

Send wedding invitations

At least two months prior to your wedding day, send wedding invitations with additional information for your guests. Some destination wedding couples choose formal invitations from a stationery store, while others choose a theme related to the destination spot. If your invitations will be more casual, consider some creative wording such as: "Please join us in presence or in spirit as we celebrate our marriage." This wording helps to emphasize that attending your destination is not mandatory, and that if your guests are not able to attend, they will still be able to share the moment with you from afar. Finalize your guest headcount and notify your wedding vendors of any necessary guest accommodations.

Up to 2 Months Prior

Check In With Guests

Call your guests several weeks prior to your destination wedding to see if they have any last-minute questions and to ask if they need any help with travel arrangements. This personalized check-in will not only help you to execute a successful wedding, but it will also help your guests feel more valued and excited to be part of your unique wedding. You may also want to send your guests a Destination Wedding Guest Checklist to help them with their travel plans.

Destination Wedding Guest Checklist

___ Passport/Visa (if required)

___ Passport copies and travel itinerary left with a friend in case of emergency

___ Sufficient supply of medications

___ Local currency/traveler's checks/credit cards

___ Photo ID for airplane boarding

___ Airline tickets

___ Hotel confirmation number

___ Rental car confirmation number

___ Clothes and toiletries

___ Comfortable shoes

___ Voltage converter (if required)

___ Sign-up for airline Frequent Flyer program (if desired)

___ Book, radio, or activity for entertainment while traveling

___ Ask a neighbor to collect mail and keep an eye on home

___ Camera

___ Destination contact information (airline phone number, hotel phone number)

___ Guide books and maps

___ Children's toys (if traveling with kids)

Check In With Wedding Vendors

Continue to be a P.E.S.T. and confirm again with your wedding coordinator, vendors, airline, and hotel. Make certain that all details are attended to, that you have gone through the necessary steps to secure your marriage license, and that your wedding day will go according to plan.

Plan Your Ceremony

If you will be writing vows, asking loved ones to read a meaningful passage, or incorporate traditions or local customs into your wedding ceremony. Finalize these details a few weeks prior to your wedding day.

Plan Your Rehearsal Dinner

If you will be hosting a rehearsal dinner the night before your wedding day, make certain that menus are confirmed and your ceremony location is available.

Say "Thank You!"

Your wedding guests have taken time off from work, traveled a far distance, and spent their own money to watch you get married. Throughout your destination wedding trip, continuously thank your guests for participating in your unique wedding and show your gratitude for their time and generosity. You may want to consider purchasing small gifts to place in your guests' hotel rooms when they arrive. A small bottle of wine and mixed nuts, along with a personalized thank you note, would add a special touch to your destination wedding.

Destination Wedding Checklist

6 Months to 1 Year Ahead:

__ Plan your budget

__ Select a destination and date

__ Finalize your guest list

__ Send "Save the Date" notices

4 to 6 Months Ahead:

__ Finalize wedding contracts

__ Decide on wedding attire

__ Plan a post-wedding celebration

2 to 4 Months Ahead:

__ Create your guest itinerary

__ Send destination wedding invitations and guest checklist

Up to 2 Months Ahead:

__ Check in with guests

__ Check in with wedding vendors

__ Plan your ceremony

__ Plan your rehearsal dinner

__ Say thank you!

Unique Wedding Spotlight: Overseas Destination Wedding

When Sara Shuman, an art designer from California, traveled through Europe many years before meeting her husband, Peter Duke, she was captivated by the beauty of Santorini, Greece. A breathtaking island with shimmering cliffs overlooking the Aegean Sea, Santorini was the spot where Sara dreamed of someday getting married.

Years later, when Sara met Peter and they decided to get married, images of a Santorini wedding still lingered. "When I thought of places to get married, I knew that I wanted a spot that would provide a beautiful backdrop for photographs. Santorini provided this setting." Sara and Peter began planning their destination wedding about four months prior to their wedding date in October of 2000. Here are some of the steps they took:

Step 1. Consider your reasons.

When contemplating her wedding options, Sara decided against a traditional wedding for three primary reasons: First, she is a creative thinker and wanted a wedding that would capture her originality. "I'm always one to think out-of-the-box and do things differently," said Sara. Her second reason for choosing a destination wedding was to avoid the costs associated with a traditional wedding. "The price of weddings is outrageous and you just don't get much," said Sara, after researching a traditional wedding option. The final reason Sara and Peter chose a destination wedding was to provide a neutral location that would not offend or inconvenience certain family members. Sara's family lives in the U.S. Virgin Islands, while Peter's family resides in California. Each family wanted the couple's wedding to be held nearer to them, but the couple did not think it was fair to require one family to travel and not another. To avoid turf wars, Sara and Peter decided to ask their family to fly to Santorini for a wedding away.

Step 2. Notify guests.

While Sara was looking forward to a dream-come-true destination wedding in Greece, her loved ones did not as eagerly embrace the idea of a non-traditional wedding. Peter's mother wanted a big, traditional wedding in California with many friends and acquaintances. She had attended many of her friends' children's weddings and believed that now those people should be guests at her son's wedding. Sara's family did not like to travel, particularly far distances. "Overall, they hated the idea," said Sara, after calling her family members to notify them of her plans. Nonetheless, Sara and Peter pushed forward with their plans for a destination wedding to Greece.

Step 3. Investigate marriage requirements.

Committed to their destination wedding idea, Sara and Peter researched the island of Santorini and made initial wedding plans. The village in which they married was so quaint that the mayor of the town was also the wedding coordinator! Sara checked into available wedding dates, airfare rates, and marriage requirements for a wedding over-seas. She also selected a hotel from a Website which al-lowed her a 360-degree virtual tour of the location.

Trying to be accommodating to her family's needs, she told her family of her chosen destination, suggested several possible wedding dates, and asked for family feedback—a big mistake, Sara later realized. Everyone had an opinion about the wedding. Peter's mother did not like Greece. Sara's family could not agree on a wedding date. There were ar-guments about logistics, costs, and wedding day details. Like traditional weddings, this destination wedding was starting to take on a life of its own and Sara and Peter were losing control.

Step 4. Stay focused.

Peter and Sara were determined to experience the type of wedding that was most meaningful to them, so they re-gained control of their wedding plans. After hearing so many criticisms and opinions from the loved ones they tried des-perately to include in the planning, the couple gave up. "After a couple of weeks of going back and forth with ev-eryone, I uninvited them to the wedding," said Sara.

The couple finalized a wedding date with the hotel and wedding coordinator and booked their flights. "I told the family that we would love them to come to our wedding, but not to come if it would be a financial or time strain. I said this is the date, this is where we will be, and these are the prices." Realizing that the couple was prepared to go it alone and that guest input was no longer valued, Peter and Sara's family quickly backed down and made their hotel and flight reservations.

Step 5. Finalize wedding day details.

Now that they were back in charge of their wedding and their loved ones were silenced, Sara and Peter finalized their wedding plans. The most important planning step, they realized, was to allow the local wedding coordinators to handle most of the details. The coordinators told Peter and Sara what they needed to bring for a marriage license and asked for any special requests, but the couple left most of the planning to the locals.

A few weeks prior to the wedding, Sara purchased a wedding gown. While most of her wedding would be unique and non-traditional, it was important to Sara to have a traditional white gown. Her dress, which won wedding-dress-of-the-month by Wholly Matrimony (*www.whollymatrimony.com*), added the final touch to her wedding day planning.

Step 6. Enjoy the experience.

Allowing the residents of Santorini to plan their destination wedding was well worth it to Sara and Peter. Not only did they not have to worry about every detail, they also experienced a wedding day unlike any other. Carried by donkeys for 20 minutes through the village, the couple made their way to the altar with all of the townspeople looking on. Local fiddlers serenaded the couple as the mayor of the town married the Peter and Sara with 14 family members looking on. Fireworks were then launched to celebrate the couple's union! By delegating control of their destination wedding planning to the coordinators in Santorini, Peter and Sara enjoyed an authentic village wedding beyond their wildest dreams.

Step 7. Schedule some "alone" time.

Sara and Peter knew that they wanted their loved ones to witness their wedding, but they also knew that they would want some private time as a couple during their trip. After the ceremony, the couple and their guests enjoyed a delicious dinner. Then, Peter and Sara left for a mini-honeymoon to Crete while their family members enjoyed the final days of a vacation in Santorini.

Step 8. Host post-wedding celebrations.

The day after their wedding ceremony, prior to departing for Crete, Sara and Peter hosted a luncheon for their guests. "I wanted to say thank you for coming all this way," said Sara. She gave each guest a wrapped gift and handed out silly prizes for who flew the farthest, who was the best photographer, and so forth. This provided a special ending to the wedding week.

While Peter and Sara were content with their destination wedding, Peter's mother insisted on planning a post-wedding celebration for her friends back in California. Peter's family planned and paid for the dinner, which was held in a famous Greek restaurant in Malibu. Sara was willing to endure the dinner because it was important to her mother-in-law and because Sara and Peter already had their perfect wedding.

Step 9. Prepare for the aftermath.

Because most of the criticism of their non-traditional wedding occurred in the early days of planning, the aftermath of the couple's wedding was rather uneventful. There were some surprises, though. "Everyone had the time of their lives," said Sara. "They all keep asking when we will return for an anniversary trip because they want to go back!" Although the couple married in 2000, the wedding lives on. "Because everyone was involved and had so much fun, the wedding memories really haven't died," said Sara. You can visit Sarah and Peter's wedding Wensite at www.idomemories.com

Tips for Other Destination Wedding Couples

1. If you have preconceived ideas of what a wedding should be, then don't do a destination wedding. If you really want your flowers to look a certain way or your ceremony to be conducted in a certain format, consider another wedding option. Destination weddings work well if you are creative, flexible, and willing to experience the local culture of your wedding destination.

2.   **When deciding on a destination, look at allied countries and places where the dollar is good.** You can get great deals on a destination wedding.

3.   **Don't coordinate other people's travel.** This can cause a lot of hassle and frustration and can make you feel responsible if guests have travel difficulties.

4.   **If you plan a destination wedding where you and your guests stay at the same hotel, consider staying in another hotel** following your ceremony or plan a brief "honeymoon" to allow for some private time.

5.   **Say thank you!** Your guests will travel great distances to see you get married. Find a special way to show them how appreciative you are.

$ *Sara and Peter's Destination Wedding Details* $

Wedding day details arranged by local wedding coordinators, including flowers, fireworks, music, donkeys, officiant, photographer, and reception dinner	= $2,500
Hotel, first-class airfare, and "honeymoon" in Crete	= $7,500
Total cost	= $10,000
Total planning time	= 4 months
Total guests	= 14

Resources for Getting Married in Greece

I Do Greece—The wedding coordinator that Sara and Peter used, Markos Karvounis, can take care of all of your

Santorini wedding details from donkeys to décor. *www.idogreece.com*

Hotel Esperas—The luxury hotel where Sara, Peter, and their guests stayed. *www.esperas.com*

Santorini Travel Website—Information on Santorini culture, accommodations, and activities, as well as detailed information on how to get married in Santorini. *www.santorini.com*

Go Greece—A comprehensive Website, featuring news, travel information, destination guides and resources for all parts of Greece. *www.gogreece.com*

Greek Tourism Office—The official Website of the Greek National Tourism Organization. *(Click on the british flag in the upper right corner to view the site in English!)www.gnto.gr*

Unique Wedding Spotlight: Last-Minute Destination Wedding

While Sara Shuman and Peter Duke took four months to plan their destination wedding to Greece, Michele Cobb and Christopher Theisen took only four days to plan their destination wedding to the coast of Maine. Michele and Christopher met during college and began a long-distance relationship while Christopher was stationed with the army in Germany.

During a two-week military leave, Michele and Christopher decided to take a trip from Delaware to Maine, where they had attended college. Originally meant to be only a nostalgic vacation, this excursion turned into a romantic and memorable destination wedding. Here are the steps Michele and Christopher took to plan their last-minute destination wedding:

Step 1. Make initial inquiries.

While driving up the East Coast, the couple started contemplating a last-minute wedding. The uncertainty of

Christopher's schedule, and the opportunity to get married in a spot that was meaningful to both of them, led Michele, a sales manager for the British Broadcasting Corporation, and Christopher to make some investigative calls to find out what it might take to marry during their trip to New England. From the road, Christopher called the Portland city hall and learned that there was a three-day waiting period for a marriage license, which worked out well for the couple. They learned that they would need to file an "intent to get married form" and then they would receive a list of justices of the peace who would marry them once the marriage license was ready. They also learned that they would need two witnesses to their marriage.

Step 2. Invite guests.

Passing through New Hampshire on their way to Maine, the couple stopped to visit Michele's parents, inform them of their wedding plans, and ask if they would be available to be the couple's witnesses. While taken aback by the couple's intentions, and concerned that it would set a bad precedent for Michele's younger siblings, Michele's parents agreed to meet the couple in Portland for the wedding.

Telling Christopher's mother and stepfather was not as easy. Because they live in California, and the couple was informing them only four days in advance of the wedding, it did not seem possible that they would be able to attend. While his mother was disheartened at the news and urged the couple to plan a "real" wedding at some future date, Christopher's parents were able to catch a last-minute flight to the East to be part of the celebration. Like with a traditional wedding, involving guests in the celebration led to some unsolicited demands and opinions. For example, the parents insisted that Michele have a bouquet; that she wear something old, new, borrowed, and blue; and that the couple exchange wedding bands. While it added slightly to their planning process, Michele and Christopher were happy to compromise on these simple details.

Step 3. Make final arrangements.

Because Michele and Christopher were not originally planning to exchange wedding rings, or do anything particularly extravagant, they needed to attend to these details prior to their wedding day.

First, upon arriving at their wedding destination, the couple applied for their marriage license and met with the justice of the peace who would perform their ceremony.

Next, they contacted Tiffany's, where Michele's engagement ring was purchased, to find out if they had any retail stores in Maine that could supply matching wedding bands. They found a jewelry store that carried Tiffany rings and selected simple bands that matched the engagement ring and could be available within three days. "The jewelry store clerks commented that we were the calmest couple they had ever seen!" said Michele.

Then, the couple purchased their wedding attire. Christopher wore a suite and Michele purchased a little navy-blue DKNY dress.

Finally, the couple made arrangements to spend their wedding night at an elegant inn in Maine to celebrate their marriage.

Step 4. Enjoy the moment.

The morning of the wedding, Michele and Christopher dressed in their wedding attire and left for the justice of the peace's office, located in an old, traditional New England–style home. The parents arrived—a huge bouquet in tow, plus all the necessities for something old, something new, something borrowed, and something blue. The guests took photographs on the front lawn of the house, and then went inside for a quick ceremony. The bride and groom and their guests ate lunch at a local restaurant and then the couple retreated to their "bridal suite."

Step 5. Deal with the aftermath.

Christopher left for Germany the day after the couple's wedding and the parents surprised the couple at the airport to see him off. The parents had some difficulty telling their family members and friends about the last-minute destination wedding, and ultimately the couple gave in to a second, breakfast wedding celebration a year later at the Harvard Club of Boston with 60 guests. "Everyone was happy to see me in the fancy dress and to eat their slice of wedding cake," said Michele. After being able to share their wedding moment as they chose, Michele and Christopher were much more content to allow their guests to revel in a more formal, post-wedding celebration.

"Ironically, my mother had initially been concerned that I would set a bad example for my siblings, and indeed I did," said Michele. After hearing about Michele and Christopher's unique wedding, Michele's brother and his wife decided to plan a destination wedding with their parents!

Tips for Other Last-Minute Destination Wedding Couples

1. The important thing to remember is that you don't need a lot of time to plan a wedding if you are willing to be a bit flexible and keep it simple. Planning a last-minute destination wedding can be easy and cost-effective. "It means you can really do what you want without having to meet the expectations of family and friends," said Michele.

2. Plan a big party or second wedding later if the family insists. This is generally easy to plan and takes the pressure off of you. As Michele suggests: "You may be nervous about what the caterer will serve or if the flowers will arrive on time, but you won't have to be worried about your personal nerves on that day."

$ **Michele and Christopher's Wedding Details** $	
Flowers	= $100
Ceremony/Officiant	= $200
Bride's wedding attire	= $200
Groom's wedding attire	= $200
Photography	= Provided free by guests
Wedding night hotel	= $200
Music	= None
Wedding announcements	= None
Post-wedding lunch	= $200
Total cost	= $1,100
Total planning time	= 4 Days
Total guests	= 4

Destination Wedding Resources

Books

The Most Romantic Resorts for Destination Weddings, Marriage Renewals and Honeymoons by Paulette Cooper and Paul Noble (SPI Books, 2002). A comprehensive guide for planning a destination wedding at popular resorts around the world, this book provides reviews from couples who married or honeymooned at 150 resort destinations, available wedding packages and costs, and contact information.

Modern Bride Honeymoons and Weddings Away: The Complete Guide to Planning Your Most Romantic Trip Ever by Geri Bain (John Wiley and Sons, 1995). While this book focuses primarily on selecting a romantic honeymoon spot and planning for the honeymoon, its tips and suggestions can be helpful to couples planning a destination wedding.

100 Best Romantic Resorts of the World (4th edition) by Katharine Dyson (Globe Pequot Press, 2002). While not geared directly towards destination weddings, this book spotlights many romantic locations around the world to host a memorable destination wedding.

Here Comes the Guide—A colossal resource for couples planning a wedding in California and Hawaii, this guide offers a directory of local vendors, wedding locations, and resources. Three guides are available: one for Northern California, one for Southern California, and one for Hawaii. You can purchase the guide at Amazon.com, or visit their Website at: *www.herecomestheguide.com/*.

Internet Resources

Wedding Channel.com (*www.weddingchannel.com*)—While targeted at traditional brides and grooms, the Wedding Channel Website has a detailed section on planning a destination wedding, including informational articles, chat rooms, and destination suggestions. You can also create your own free Website to inform your guests of important details or to share interesting facts about your wedding destination.

The Knot.com—Like Wedding Channel.com, The Knot caters primarily to traditional brides and grooms but offers an array of resources for unique couples, including planning tips, "real-life" destination wedding stories, and a question-and-answer forum. *www.theknot.com*

Wyndham Resorts—A respected international hotel chain, Wyndham caters to couples who want to plan a destination wedding. *www.destinationweddingsbywyndham.com*

Sandals Resorts—A highly respected, all-inclusive travel company, Sandals specializes in Caribbean destination weddings and will cater to every detail of your wedding day celebration—including complimentary his and hers "Just Married" T-shirts! Also, if you stay for a week at one of their resorts, your wedding celebration is free. *www.sandals.com*

Destination Weddings and Honeymoons magazine—This Website features articles and helpful links for destination wedding couples to supplement the semi-annual publication of this new magazine. *www.islands.com/weddings/magazine*

Chapter 7

Surprise Weddings

Picture this: Your guests arrive for a summertime party with friends. They bring their coolers and potato salad and look forward to an afternoon of sunshine and laughter. After everyone arrives and the good cheer grows, you clink a glass to get the group's attention. All sunglasses turn to you as you announce, "Surprise! We're getting married today and you're our guests!"

If you are like many couples, you value being surrounded by friends and family members on your wedding day, but you want to avoid the annoyances and frustrations of planning a traditional wedding. By thinking "out-of-the-box" beyond the traditional wedding prototype, you realize that you *can* have your wedding cake and eat it too!

Many couples are choosing this no-hassle, family-oriented wedding option. Eric Clapton, for example, married his wife Melia McEnery on New Year's Day in 2002 by surprising his guests. Friends and loved ones had arrived at a church to see the Christening of Clapton's daughters. After the ceremony, the priest called the couple to the altar and joined them in holy matrimony—much to the surprise of the guests! But surprise weddings are not just for famous rock musicians who want to avoid the limelight. Many "real-life" couples are choosing this wedding option to create a memorable day for loved ones without having to dote over traditional wedding details.

You may want to plan a surprise wedding if:

> You want to be surrounded by friends and family on your wedding day.

> You like the idea of a traditional wedding without the aggravation.

> You want your guests to be relaxed and to enjoy themselves.

> You want to save money.

> You want to incorporate some traditional wedding customs but avoid most of the pomp and circumstance of a typical wedding.

> You like to be in control of your wedding day details.

> You want minimal planning and stress.

> You want your wedding to occur within a few months.

> You can keep a secret!

Pros and Cons

Next to elopements, surprise weddings can be the easiest to plan and require only a couple months of lead time—to make certain your invitations reach those you are hoping will attend. While the level of planning—and costs—will vary depending on the type of surprise wedding you plan, the stress and responsibility are very minimal. With just a few phone calls to reserve a tent or purchase a cake, you are ready to have a wedding that is as unique as you are and fun for everyone. Unsuspecting guests, who think they are coming to an engagement party, your annual holiday open house, or a birthday bash, may be pleasantly surprised to learn that you have orchestrated a surprise wedding day. They often arrive dressed casually (unless otherwise instructed), without the burden of gifts or feelings of obligation. If they are attending a party at your home or in another informal location, they will often ask if they can bring food or beverages, which defrays your costs and gets them involved.

One of the greatest benefits of surprise weddings is their versatility. They can be elaborate celebrations with caterers, musicians, and formalwear, or they can be casual weekend get-togethers. Surprise weddings are also a great choice for couples who are leaning towards a traditional wedding but who want to avoid its pressures and irritations. You could easily go through the planning steps involved with organizing a traditional wedding but keep your plans a secret to friends and loved ones. Without the endless opinions and confrontations of traditional wedding planning, you will be able to plan the traditional wedding you want— stress-free.

If you ask traditional wedding couples what their greatest source of stress was, they likely won't say that it was dealing with the photographer or the florist. Most wedding planning stress originates from demanding in-laws, sensitive bridesmaids, and arguments about costs and formalities. If you plan a traditional wedding without guest input, you will be in total control of your celebration and will enjoy plotting your day with your partner. You will be able to have *your* traditional wedding. When they arrive at your party venue, your guests will likely be amazed that you were able to plan a traditional wedding on your own. They will also enjoy a more relaxed celebration without the puppetry of a traditional wedding and will fondly reminisce about the occasion for years to come.

Perhaps the biggest drawback of any type of surprise wedding is the fact that it is a surprise, and secrets often get out. When you choose a surprise wedding, be very careful about whom you tell and when. Too many couples get talked out of this magical wedding experience because loved ones discover the secret too soon and convince couples that a traditional wedding is the better choice. Make certain that you and your partner are committed to this wedding choice and have formulated a solid defense before sharing the news with loved ones. Also, be certain to explain to your wedding vendors (caterer, photographer, florist, DJ, officiant, stationery store clerk, and so on) that your wedding will be a surprise. Vendors often work with your friends and acquaintances and your secret could easily get leaked if you don't warn your wedding vendors of your intentions.

Another significant drawback to a surprise wedding is disappointment if some friends and family members are not able to join you. Surprise weddings are a great choice for couples whose guests live close by and can easily meet for a party. If your loved ones are scattered throughout the country or around the world, it might be more difficult to get them to attend your celebration without raising suspicion. While it may cause some challenges, distance does not need to halt your surprise wedding plans. You may need to be flexible with dates and venues and plan a wedding at a time when most family members and friends are available or in town. Holidays, birthdays, baptisms, and anniversary parties are great excuses to get loved ones together. You could also plan a reunion and call far-away relatives and friends personally to ask them to attend. Recognize, though, that because you will be inviting guests to a party, not a wedding, they may not feel as obligated to attend. You may decide to disclose your wedding plans to some of these guests to urge them to attend, but again be careful that your surprise wedding doesn't lose its "surprise" factor.

There is another surprise wedding solution for couples hoping to avoid a traditional wedding reception but who want to celebrate with family members and friends that may live far away and will need some lead time to attend a surprise wedding party. Plan a small wedding ceremony with a handful of immediate family members and then surprise remaining friends and family members with a post-wedding celebration. You and your close loved ones could enjoy a quiet ceremony in a church or courthouse, and then celebrate over a simple brunch or dinner. Then, as you and your spouse depart for your honeymoon, you slip your wedding announcements in the mail along with an invitation to a post-wedding celebration to be held several weeks later. This way, you enjoy your wedding ceremony with the people who are most important to you, and you celebrate later with friends and family members who are scattered around the globe.

Surprise Wedding Trade-Offs

Pros	Cons
They can be casual and relaxed or formal and traditional.	They can be disappointing if some loved ones are not able to attend.
They can be combined with another unique wedding option, such as a Theme Wedding.	Not ideal if loved ones are geographically scattered.
They can involve many friends and loved ones.	The secret may get out.
They can be inexpensive.	They can cause family upsets.
They can be planned quickly and easily at any time during the year.	They can turn into traditional weddings if too many people find out.
Guests don't feel obligated to purchase gifts or act in a certain way.	They can require some flexibility with location, food, officiant, and entertainment.

Planning Tips

While surprise weddings are generally straightforward and effortless, there are certain planning considerations to be aware of to make your wedding day a success.

1. Decide How to Hoodwink Your Friends

Your biggest challenge when planning a surprise wedding will likely be the "surprise" part. How will you woo your friends and family members to attend a party without mounting suspicion? Fortunately for you, most of your loved ones won't even comprehend that you would plan a non-traditional wedding, so you can use your uniqueness to your advantage. Still, you need to find a way to gather guests together at a location and time that is convenient for you and them. Many surprise wedding couples choose to piggyback their wedding on top of another event to reduce suspicion. If you or a friend typically hosts a Fourth of July party or an Easter brunch, consider using this occasion to host your wedding. If you or a loved one will be celebrating a milestone birthday or anniversary, ask if you can join in the fun.

You may want your wedding to be separate from other events throughout the year. If so, plan a dinner party or an engagement party. Tell the bride and groom's family members that you would like them to get to know each other better and plan a weekend retreat. If something exciting is going on in your town during a certain part of the year, such as an annual country fair or a high-profile sporting event, then consider inviting guests to join you for the occasion.

You have many options for deceiving your friends and loved ones. Sit down as a couple to select your approach and then let the planning begin!

2. Choose Your Surprise Wedding Style

One of the great benefits of a surprise wedding is that it can be as formal or casual as you choose. You could decide to plan a traditional wedding ceremony and reception unbeknownst to your guests, or you could plan a simple ceremony with an informal party. Decide together what is important to you as a couple and how much you want to spend. Do you want a large wedding with more than 100 guests? Or would you like a more intimate occasion? Do you want your guests to be dressed formally or are shorts and a T-shirt okay? Do you want fancy food and spirits? Or are hamburgers and beer acceptable? These are some of the questions to ask to help you think about the style of wedding that is right for you.

3. Select a Décor

If you would like to plan a more "traditional" non-traditional wedding, then select an appropriate venue and inform guests in invitations that formalwear is requested. Planning a traditional, surprise wedding around a New Year's Eve celebration, cocktail party, or holiday get-together can help to avoid red-flags regarding formal wear or an elegant venue. If your surprise wedding will be more casual, then decide where you would like to host this event, the type of food and entertainment you want, and what you would like your guests to wear and bring.

4. Decide Whom to Tell

As with elopements, you run the risk of losing control of your surprise wedding when you choose to disclose your plans to friends and loved ones. Just telling a mother or a sister can frequently lead to an explosion of opinion and a secret spread far and wide! That said, many surprise wedding couples choose to tell a few close loved ones of their plans to solicit help and support. Make certain that the people you choose to tell of your plans will embrace your ideas and not discourage your efforts. You will also need to be prepared to firmly state your wedding wishes and explain what role, if any, you are expecting your loved ones to perform.

5. Confirm Wedding Day Details

Surprise weddings are best planned at least a couple of months in advance, particularly if you need to reserve a venue or tent rental, find a caterer and entertainment, and purchase invitations and decorations. If your surprise wedding will be more traditional, then you may want to start your planning at least six months prior to your wedding day. If your surprise wedding will be a small affair or will be affixed to another occasion, then you may have the luxury of doing very little planning and can wait until the last minute. Once you select your surprise wedding style and venue, find an officiant who will accommodate your unique wedding. Many celebrants may be booked during popular summer months, may not want to travel to certain venues, or may be unwilling to give up a holiday to marry you. The more lead time you allow yourself, the better your chances of finding an officiant who suits your needs.

6. Select Your Wedding Attire

If your surprise wedding will be traditional or formal, then purchase (or rent) your wedding attire at least a couple of months prior to your wedding day. If you will be wearing something more casual, you may decide to purchase a new skirt or shirt and will want to start shopping for your outfit. If you decide to have a wedding party, and have informed your bridesmaids and ushers of your plans, then finalize their wedding attire more than two months prior to your wedding day to allow time for fittings and alterations. Or use some of the online wedding attire resources presented in this book to cut down on time pressures and hassles.

7. Invite Your Guests

Unlike a typical party, a surprise wedding requires inviting guests further in advance to ensure they can attend.

Two months prior to your wedding day is a good time to send out invitations, so you will want to purchase them or have them printed previously. Depending on the type of surprise wedding you are planning, your invitations may lead to suspicion. If guests ask why you sent out invitations at all—or so far in advance—simply state that you know it can be a busy time of the year and you are hoping for a good turnout. Sending more casual invitations that don't look like typical wedding stationery might be a good way to distract suspicious relatives.

8. Plan the Surprise

When and how will you reveal your secret to your guests? Some surprise wedding couples who choose a more formal wedding may hide until their guests arrive. Bridesmaids and ushers distribute wedding programs to astonished guests, while you and your partner watch your guests' expressions from a clandestine spot. Or maybe you decide to join in on the greetings. If your surprise wedding is more casual than a traditional style, you may mingle with your unknowing guests until your officiant arrives. Then you or a loved one gathers your guests together to announce the start of your wedding ceremony. Whether formal or informal, your surprise wedding is sure to be a fun occasion for you and your guests.

9. Prepare for the Aftermath

Most of your guests will be delighted by your unique surprise wedding and happy that they were included in your special day. They will recognize the true meaning of your wedding—a time for family and friends to witness your union—without the materialistic components that characterize many traditional weddings. Be aware, however, that some of your guests may be disappointed by your covert nuptials. Loved ones may be upset that they were not able to help you plan your traditional wedding and may feel that you intentionally deceived them. Other friends and family members may be taken aback by this non-traditional wedding option and may need some time to realize how special and enjoyable the experience was. In time, most of your friends and relatives will accept your unique wedding and may question why they didn't think of something so fun!

Surprise Wedding Ideas

- Backyard barbecue.
- Beach/pool party.
- Annual holiday party.
- New Year's Eve gathering.
- Halloween party.
- Birthday party.
- Graduation party.
- Family reunion.
- Family vacation.
- Trip to a local park or museum.
- Friday night dinner at a favorite restaurant.
- Wedding shower/engagement party-turned-wedding.
- Cocktail party with friends.
- House-warming party.
- Meet-the-family party.
- Super Bowl party.
- Sunday brunch party.
- Bachelor and Bachelorette party-turned-wedding.

Unique Wedding Spotlight:
Surprise Barbecue Wedding

Joan and Rick Hughes knew that they wanted a unique wedding celebration that would involve their guests in a relaxed celebration. Both in their early 30s, Rick had been divorced and Joan had never been married. As Joan said, "The more I looked into the traditional wedding, the more stressed I got! I had been living on my own for 10 years and the idea of a traditional wedding just wasn't appealing. All that money for just one night—it didn't seem worth it. I'd rather have a nice house and avoid the time and stress involved with planning a more traditional wedding."

After deciding not to plan a traditional wedding, the couple looked into planning a destination wedding to a quaint country inn. They soon realized, however, that they couldn't keep the guest list down and they wanted to share their wedding with their many friends and loved ones. "We wanted everyone to show up to our wedding, be comfortable, and have a good time," said Joan. On an August day in 1991 in the couple's backyard, that's exactly what happened.

Two months prior to their wedding, Joan and Rick began planning their surprise. Here are the steps they took:

Step 1. Plan the surprise.

After deciding not to plan a traditional wedding or a destination wedding to a country inn, Rick and Joan started brainstorming other wedding options that would require very little time and aggravation. Rick announced, "What about a surprise backyard barbecue wedding?" They both loved the idea, believing that it would have all of the elements important to them for their wedding.

Step 2. Decide whom to tell.

Most of the couple's 75 wedding day guests had no idea about the couple's surprise wedding plans. They thought they were coming to a summertime cookout in the couple's backyard. But Rick and Joan wanted a few key people to know about their nuptials prior to the wedding day. In June, the couple told both sets of parents about their plans, as well as Rick's two children, Joan's sister (her maid of honor), and seven of Joan's friends. Joan had a very close group of friends and it was important to her for them to be involved with the planning.

Most of the guests who knew about the wedding plans ahead of time were thrilled with the couple's plans and eager to be involved. Joan's mom, however, was disappointed. She was hoping for a more traditional wedding and the opportunity to see Joan walk down a church aisle. Joan spent some time alone with her mother talking about the couple's wishes and the true meaning of their wedding day, and her mom eventually embraced the decision.

Step 3. Confirm wedding day details.

In the two months prior to their wedding day, Joan and Rick reserved a justice of the peace to perform the ceremony, rented a tent and some grills for their backyard, and ordered a cake from a local pastry shop. Most of their guests would bring food or beverages to the cookout, but Joan and Rick visited bulk discount stores (such as BJ's and Costco) to purchase hamburgers and hotdogs, champagne, and paper goods. They looked into hiring a caterer, but the cost was high and it would have created a more formal atmosphere that the couple wanted to avoid.

While seeking a non-traditional wedding experience, Joan and Rick decided to sprinkle in some wedding traditions. Joan and her bridesmaids planned a bachelorette party, and on the day of her wedding, her friends showered her with something old, new, borrowed, and blue. The couple also chose to follow tradition by planning a bouquet and garter toss during their celebration.

Step 4. Purchase wedding attire.

When their guests arrived for the barbecue, Rick and Joan were dressed casually in shorts and a t-shirt. They had purchased some fancier clothes for their wedding celebration and changed into their wedding attire just prior to the ceremony. Joan purchased a white silk skirt, white blouse, and white shoes. Rick purchased a new shirt and trousers.

Step 5. Invite guests.

One month prior to their wedding, Rick and Joan purchased pre-printed cookout invitations at a local stationery store and sent them out to their friends and family members. Most of their loved ones lived nearby, which made planning this type of wedding easier and more successful. Only a few friends were unable to attend.

Step 6. Announce the surprise!

After all their guests arrived and the justice of the peace showed up, Joan and Rick retreated to the house to change into their wedding attire. When the bride and groom were ready, Joan's sister gathered everyone into a circle and announced that Joan and Rick had a surprise for them. Then, the justice of the peace appeared and Joan's mother walked Joan out of the house and towards the officiant, where Rick stood. The guests cheered with excitement! After the celebrant announced them husband and wife, Rick and Joan joined their guests in a champagne toast and enjoyed the remaining hours of their surprise wedding barbecue surrounded by their favorite people.

Step 7. Be prepared for the aftermath.

Most of their guests thought their surprise backyard wedding was a great idea. They agreed with Joan and Rick that the purpose of a wedding was to have fun with loved ones, not to be showered with gifts and obey tradition. Many guests remarked that they would have loved to plan a similar wedding. But some guests thought they had missed out on something and were perplexed at this unusual wedding. One friend asked Joan, "You didn't want to walk down the aisle and be the belle of the ball?" Joan responded: "I'm the belle in the backyard!" Other guests thought the surprise wedding "broke the rules" and was somehow egregious. While Joan was disappointed by their reactions, she took their criticisms with a grain of salt. "They did the traditional wedding and several of them are divorced, while we are still married. It's kind of ironic."

Tips For Other Surprise Wedding Couples

1. **Do what you want to do.** "When you plan a traditional wedding, you're planning it for everyone else but yourself. Do what *you* want," say Joan and Rick. Clearly express your wedding wishes and stay committed to your plans. Everyone will eventually support your decision.

2. **Get your guests involved.** Rick and Joan kept costs down by asking guests to contribute to the barbecue fare. Encouraging guests to bring food, beverages, or paper goods to your backyard wedding also helps guests to play a more integral role in your wedding celebration. By involving their guests in their surprise wedding, Rick and Joan were able to host their entire wedding for only $750.

3. **Don't expect gifts.** When you plan a surprise wedding, you are implicitly choosing a wedding that does not involve wedding gifts and related obligations. While some loved ones will undoubtedly send you a post-wedding present, you should not expect material gain from your surprise wedding. "The purpose of this type of wedding is to have fun with friends and loved ones, not to have gifts," says Joan.

Unique Wedding Spotlight:
Surprise Oceanside Wedding

After getting engaged at the base of Mount Washington in New Hampshire's White Mountains, Sarah and Tom Long decided to plan a wedding that would capture their independent spirit and ingenuity. "Some girls dream about a wedding with a big white dress. That was never my dream," says Sarah, a meteorologist. Instead of a traditional wedding, Sarah and Tom planned a surprise wedding ceremony on the cliff of Portland Head Light, a historic lighthouse off the Maine coast, and a spiritual spot for Tom and Sarah. "Tom goes to Portland Head Light every Sunday," says Sarah. "It's like his church." While their surprise wedding was a simple occasion with only a few guests, the couple began their planning two months prior to their wedding day. Here are some of the steps they took to prepare for their surprise wedding:

Step 1. Select the wedding date.

Sarah and Tom wanted to get married in the presence of a few close family members, but avoid the expectations and obligations of a traditional wedding. A surprise wedding seemed like the perfect solution for this creative couple. They decided that they would invite a few close family members over to their apartment on a Saturday in July, and surprise them with a pre-planned wedding.

Step 2. Be firm with vendors.

Most of the wedding planning was flawless, except for ordering the flowers. Sarah arrived at the flower shop to order her simple bouquet. She explained that she was having a quiet, outdoor wedding ceremony with just a few close family members. "All of a sudden I had all of these flower books in front of me," says Sarah. "Their idea of a simple bouquet cost $200!" After asserting her wedding plans more clearly, and asking specifically for a small bouquet of long-stemmed daisies, Sarah ended up with the $30 bouquet she adored.

Step 3. Invite guests.

After the flowers were ordered, Sarah and Tom reserved a justice of the peace and purchased a new skirt for Sarah and a new shirt for Tom to wear on their wedding day. The only remaining details were to invite the guests and plan the announcement. Three weeks prior to the wedding day, Sarah called her sister and brother-in-law, and Tom called his sister and brother to invite them over to their apartment for a get-together. "We told them that we hadn't seen them in awhile and we wanted to have everyone get to know each other better and have some fun," said Sarah.

After the guest list was confirmed, Tom, a talented artist, drew the couple's wedding announcement and had color copies printed at a local print shop to be sent to friends and family following their surprise wedding.

Step 4. Announce the surprise!

When their four guests arrived at Sarah and Tom's apartment, they gathered in the living room and announced, "We have a bit of a surprise. We're not just hanging out for the day. We're getting married and you're our witnesses." Everyone was thrilled with the news and excited to be a part of the special occasion. Tom's sister did express concern for how Tom's very traditional family would take the news, but all of the wedding day guests decided to enjoy the day and deal with the aftermath later. The wedding party drove to Portland Head Light and met up with the justice of the peace who had prepared a simple, 10-minute ceremony. After the wedding, the couple treated their witnesses to lunch at a local restaurant and then drove off to Montreal for a week-long honeymoon.

Step 5. Anticipate the aftermath.

Sarah and Tom had planned to announce their wedding after returning home from Montreal, but as with many weddings—traditional or not—things don't always go as planned. While they were in Montreal, Tom's sister spilled the news to his parents. A family with staunch Irish-Catholic roots, Tom's relatives were hurt and angry by the couple's decision. It caused a lot of anxiety for Tom and a ripple in the family, who was not prepared for a non-traditional wedding. Tom and Sarah anticipated these reactions and were able to smooth out the situation somewhat by enabling Tom's mother to plan a casual, outdoor reception later that summer. "Even two years later, they're still not okay with it," says Sarah of her in-laws. "It's still a very sore subject." The negative reactions to their wedding from some family members have not, however, caused Sarah and Tom any regret. In fact, they say, that these reactions "reaffirmed why we did this."

While some family members reacted negatively to the couple's non-traditional wedding, most family members and friends had the opposite reaction. Shortly after returning from Montreal, the couple went out to dinner with Sarah's parents and her sister and brother-in-law. "I gave my sister my wedding ring before meeting my parents. In the middle of dinner, my sister said that she had an announcement to make, and said that she would now like to give me back my wedding ring." Sarah's parents were thrilled. "My parents had eloped more than 30 years ago and I think had subtly hoped that Tom and I would choose a non-traditional wedding."

Tips for Other Surprise Wedding Couples

1. **Set clear expectations of secrecy.** If you decide to announce your wedding plans to some people before others, make sure you set very clear expectations for these loved ones not to tell anyone else. But you should also anticipate that the secret may get out and be prepared to deal with the consequences.

2. **Meet your officiant prior to your wedding day.** Sarah and Tom were slightly disappointed by the generic words that their justice of the peace

presented. "He was also an older gentleman and as he was trying to climb up the cliff at the lighthouse, I was nervous that he wasn't going to make it!"

3. **Make certain that you both want a surprise wedding.** While in many ways less stressful than traditional weddings, non-traditional nuptials can still cause many challenges. Make sure that you and your partner are fully committed to a non-traditional wedding and are prepared to defend your actions. You should have no regrets.

$ *Sarah and Tom's Surprise Wedding Details* $	
Flowers	= $30
Ceremony	= $60
Wedding attire	= $50
Photography	= $20
Post-wedding lunch	= $50
Announcements	= $40
Reception	= $200
Total costs	= $450
Total planning time	= 2 Months
Total guests	= 4

Surprise Wedding Resources

If you have never planned a party for a crowd before, then here are some resources to help you get ready for a surprise wedding:

Books

Diane Warner's Great Parties on Small Budgets by Diane Warner (New Page, 2002). Learn how to plan all types of parties, from preparing the food, to decorating, to entertaining the guests.

Diane Warner's Big Book of Parties by Diane Warner (New Page, 1999). Offers creative ideas for planning a special celebration.

Cater Your Own Wedding, Revised Edition by Michael Flowers and Donna Bankhead (New Page, 2005). Shows readers how to prepare for a large party, what to serve, how much food to provide, and how to take the hassle out of wedding preparations.

Secrets from a Caterer's Kitchen, by Nicole Alani (H.P. Books, 2001). A practical book on entertaining and cooking for a crowd.

Other Resources

The Food Network—*www.foodtv.com*—Offers tips on cooking and entertaining for large groups, including menu suggestions, beverage selections, and recipes.

BJ's Wholesale Club (*www.bjs.com*), **Costco** (*www.costco.com*), and **Sam's Club** (*www.samsclub.com*)— Wholesale companies that sell food and supplies in bulk at discount prices.

Taylor Rental—A franchise company with locations nationwide, Taylor Rental supplies tents, chairs, tables, dance floors, cooking and party supplies, linens, grills, and much more! Visit *www.taylorrental.com* for a store near you.

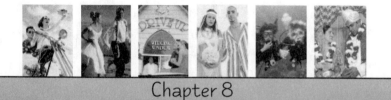

Chapter 8

Theme Weddings

Like surprise weddings, theme weddings can add a unique flare to your non-traditional wedding celebration that will keep your guests talking about your special day for years to come. Theme weddings are appealing to couples who want to add some originality and excitement to their wedding day. As with any of the creative wedding ideas discussed in this book, a theme wedding can be as outrageous or typical as you wish. Just adding a theme to a traditional wedding celebration can enliven the day, guide your planning, and create an enjoyable atmosphere for your guests. Or you can create an entirely original theme wedding without any traditional accoutrements. If you want a fun wedding day that actively involves your guests and is filled with many laughs and candid moments, then a theme wedding may be the perfect option. This chapter helps you choose a wedding theme, offers tips for planning one of six popular theme weddings, and shares "real-life" theme wedding stories of couples who chose to say I do with a twist.

You may want to plan a theme wedding if:

> You want to be surrounded by friends and family on your wedding day.

> You want your guests to have a great time at your wedding.

> You are creative and flexible.

> You want minimal planning and stress.

> You want a formal event without traditional wedding hassles.

> You want a casual party that involves all guests.

> You want to save money.

> You have guests who are up for anything.

Choose Your Wedding Theme

Like with most non-traditional wedding planning, you don't need many months to plan your day. But there are a few steps to take to make sure your day is a success. The first step in planning a theme wedding is to choose the type of theme that interests you. To help you select a theme, take a moment to complete the Theme Wedding Survey with your partner.

Theme Wedding Survey

To get you thinking about possible theme wedding ideas, rate how interested you are in each of the following party themes: (5=very interested, 1= not interested)

1. Christmas/Holiday
(Santa, lights, carols, snowflakes):   5   4   3   2   1
2. Halloween
(costumes, haunted house):   5   4   3   2   1
3. Tropical/Hawaiian
(luau, beach, pineapple):   5   4   3   2   1

4. Murder Mystery
(suspense, games): 5 4 3 2 1

5. Patriotic
(red, white, and blue, July 4th): 5 4 3 2 1

6. Cinderella
(Disney World, fairy tale, castles): 5 4 3 2 1

7. Irish (Guinness, claddagh, celtic
crosses St. Patrick's Day, shamrocks): 5 4 3 2 1

8. Asian (fortune cookies, takeout,
kimonos, sushi, Chinese New Year): 5 4 3 2 1

9. Wine Tasting
(vintner, fancy appetizers): 5 4 3 2 1

10. Greek (togas, Greek food,
Athens, Olympics): 5 4 3 2 1

11. Wild West
(line dancing, cowboy hats, saloon): 5 4 3 2 1

12. Scavenger Hunt
(contests, guest involvement): 5 4 3 2 1

13. Barbecue
(grill food, outdoors, beer): 5 4 3 2 1

14. Renaissance
(court jester, peasant costumes): 5 4 3 2 1

15. Sports (Football/Baseball/
Basketball, golf, munchies, TV): 5 4 3 2 1

16. Mardi Gras (beads, hats,
noisemakers, Bourbon Street): 5 4 3 2 1

17. Clambake/Lobster Bake
(seafood, outdoors, picnics): 5 4 3 2 1

18. Casino Night (gambling,
Las Vegas, Rat Pack, Elvis): 5 4 3 2 1

19. Academy Awards (red carpet,
fancy gowns, Hollywood): 5 4 3 2 1

20. 80's Dance Club
(music, punk rock, big hair): 5 4 3 2 1

21. New Year's Eve (champagne, fancy gowns, glitter and noise):	5	4	3	2	1
22. Swing Party (dancing, big band):	5	4	3	2	1
23. Comedy Show (jokes, performances):	5	4	3	2	1
24. "Survivor" Wedding (jungle theme, contests, bathing suits, surprises):	5	4	3	2	1
25. DC Follies (guests dressed as politicians, speeches, scandal):	5	4	3	2	1

Choose a wedding theme that interests you the most and that displays your personality and creative spirit. Many theme weddings revolve around holiday celebrations. For example, if you have a Christmas party every year, why not consider turning the event into your wedding day? Everyone enjoys a New Year's Eve celebration, so why not invite your guests over for a midnight marriage? If you love Halloween, how about planning a costume-party wedding? If a holiday theme wedding doesn't interest you, there are many other choices. If you are a golf fanatic, why not tie the knot on the 18th hole? If you're a beach bum, consider a tropical wedding theme. You may even decide to combine your theme wedding with a surprise wedding or destination wedding to make the celebration even more electrifying. Your guests may think they are coming to your house for an ethnic dinner of souvlaki and baklava, and suddenly they are in your Big Fat Greek Wedding—complete with togas, of course!

Before you launch into the planning stage of your unique wedding, think about the benefits and drawbacks of a theme wedding:

Theme Wedding Trade-Offs

Pros	Cons
It can be elegant or outrageous.	It may not be ideal for younger guests.
It involves all of your guests.	It may not be fun for guests who are more reserved or traditional.
It can be planned inexpensively.	Costs may rise if festivities are held at a hotel or function hall.
It can be personalized.	Your ceremony may be overshadowed by the theme party.
There are many resources available to help you plan the event.	It can require a lot of space.

Popular Theme Wedding Planning Tips

If you decide that the benefits of a theme wedding outweigh the drawbacks, and you identify the wedding themes that most interest you, it's time to think about the details involved in planning a theme wedding. Some theme weddings take longer to plan, are more costly, and have more opportunities for things to go wrong . To help you with your planning, here are suggestions for how to plan six popular theme weddings:

Halloween Wedding Theme

A Halloween Theme Wedding can be entertaining for guests of all ages. Decorating and hosting a Halloween wedding is straightforward and inexpensive and your guests become a focal point of your day. Here are some planning tips for a Halloween theme wedding:

Step 1. Select a location.

Haunted houses, basements, and function rooms are versatile locations for a Halloween theme wedding. You might also consider an outdoor wedding with haunted hay-rides and a large bonfire to keep your guests cozy. Just re-member to contact your local fire department before your wedding day to see about bonfire restrictions!

Step 2. Order decorations and party supplies.

Black and orange are the quintessential Halloween col-ors, so you should try to purchase invitations and party sup-plies that accentuate your ghoulish theme. Candles, pumpkins, cornstalks, headstones, and skeletons are just some of the decorations you may want to incorporate into your Halloween wedding. Consider miniature engraved pumpkins for your party favors. Have your guests throw black and orange confetti after your ceremony. If you are planning your Halloween wedding close to October, then you should have no trouble finding party supplies in any local store. If your Halloween wedding is a few months away, it may take some additional legwork.

Step 3. Select your costumes.

Will your costumes be a traditional wedding gown and tuxedo, or are you going to try something more adventur-ous? At Halloween, you are free to be as unconventional as you wish. Conventional wedding attire, accented with black and orange accessories and costume jewelry, could allow you to blend the traditional with the imaginative. You may also consider a gothic theme for your wedding attire to add some creative formality to your dress. Or you and your spouse could choose a costume theme that is personalized to your individual interests and hobbies. If you both enjoy surfing, for example, why not dress in your surf gear and add a veil and bow tie to your ensembles? As for your guests, inform them in your wedding invitation that they should arrive in costume and you can include any special instructions. For example, you may ask that couples choose "his and her" complementary costumes.

Step 4. Plan your menu.

Sweets and snacks are, of course, the centerpiece of any Halloween celebration (especially candy corn), but there are many nutritious dishes that you can add to your Halloween wedding menu. Consider foods that accentuate the fall harvest, such as squashes, pumpkin, and poultry, and offer your guests warm apple cider to wash down their food. Add creative names to your dishes, such as "Toxic Tarts" or "Lethal Legumes."

Step 5. Choose your entertainment.

Halloween parties are entertaining in their own right, but if you want to really engage your guests, consider traditional Halloween entertainment, such as bobbing for apples, three-legged races, pumpkin-carving and, of course, best costume contests.

Resources for a Halloween Theme Wedding

Locations

> Salem, Massachusetts—Home of the Salem Witch Trials, Salem puts on a grand Halloween festival each October. Combine your Halloween theme wedding with a destination wedding for a truly original wedding day. *www.hauntedhappenings.org*

> Sanger, California—Haunted hayrides, enchanted forests and month-long Halloween festivities make Hobbs Grove in Sanger, California an ideal spot for your theme wedding. *www.hobbsgrove.com.*

> Las Vegas, Nevada– There's a wedding theme for everyone in Las Vegas. Visit *www.vivalasvegasweddings.com* for information on how to turn your Las Vegas wedding chapel into a ghastly graveyard.

> Nationwide—Want a Halloween wedding venue that's closer to home? Check out *www.hauntedhouse.com* for a directory of more than 200 haunted party locations by state.

Decorations and Supplies

> *Shindigz.com*—An online party supply store with a good selection of Halloween decorations and party favors.

> *Colorsbydesign.com*—A stationery store with a wide variety of inexpensive Halloween invitations that you can design online.

> *Evite.com*—Why not send an e-mail invitation to your Halloween wedding? *Evite.com* has more than a dozen electronic Halloween invitation designs to choose from.

> *Themepartiesnmore.com*—A great Website with theme party ideas and supplies.

Costumes

> *www.allcostumes.com*—Great selection of affordable and creative costumes available for online purchase, including many gothic gowns perfect for the wedding party.

> *www.buycostumes.com*—Purchase costumes, accessories, decorations, and party favors online.

Food and Entertainment

> Perfect Entertaining—For a vast selection of Halloween recipes, visit Perfect Entertaining at *www.perfectentertaining.com/halloween/*.

> *Halloween Magazine*—For Halloween wedding activities and additional resources to help you plan your unique October wedding, visit *www.halloweenmagazine.com*.

> Consider contacting a local Tarot reader for fortune-telling fun!

Casino Night Theme Wedding

If a night of poker, roulette, good food, and entertainment is in the cards for you, then you can bet on a great time! Following some simple planning steps can help you avoid losing big:

Step 1. Choose your casino night vendor.

There are many casino vendors who can set up a party casino for your wedding. They will rent you everything you need for your casino wedding to be a success, from slot machines to poker chips. Many of these vendors can even personalize your casino night. Poker chips that say "Congratulations, Bride and Groom," or play-money printed with the bride and groom's faces, can add humor and context to your special day. Tell your casino vendor that you are planning a large party for family and friends. There should be no reason to tell the vendor that your party is a wedding until after the fees are finalized.

Step 2. Decide on your wedding budget and plan.

Most casino vendors have packages that vary by price, from high-end parties that include several dealers, lights, accessories, music, and prizes, to lower-priced options. You can generally decide the types and quantity of games to include in your casino night, the number of dealers, and the décor. Find a casino vendor that will work with you and your budget to create an exciting wedding party. If you are do-it-yourselfer, then you can bypass the casino rental vendor and purchase your own casino goods to create your theme wedding. Check out party supply stores for casino supplies and decorations. But beware: the costs can escalate. Casino packages, including gaming supplies and accessories, can cost you several hundred dollars. You may be better off using a casino rental vendor who can manage all of the details for you.

Step 3. Select a wedding venue.

Many casino vendors will help you to find a venue that is accustomed to this type of party. Casino-themed weddings can take up a lot of room, so you will want to find a space that can accommodate your guests as well as your gaming tables and food. If your house, basement, or backyard is large, then these can be great spots for a casino wedding. If not, look into local function halls and hotels to host your casino wedding. Tell the rental hall that you are planning a casino night party for your family and friends, and ask if they can host it for you. Avoid the word "wedding" in your inquiries. As we have mentioned previously, any time you tell a vendor that you are planning a wedding—no matter how non-traditional—the price tag may arbitrarily rise. Give them the estimated guest count, explain the casino theme, tell them what you are looking for in terms of food, let them know if you will be having a band or DJ—but do not tell them you are having a wedding until all fees are finalized!

Step 4. Invite your guests.

Invitations to a casino theme wedding can be very fun! Most large party supply stores offer casino-themed invitations, or you can create your own using a desktop publishing program. If you prefer to save time and hassle, consider designing and purchasing your invitation on the Web using an online stationery provider. Include some play money or chips with your invitation to entice your guests! Think about the atmosphere you want to create at your casino-theme wedding, and instruct your guests to dress accordingly.

Step 5. Let the chips fall where they may!

You'll probably want your wedding ceremony to occur early in the evening before your guests get immersed in their winnings. When your officiant arrives, ask all dealers to stop, gather your guests in a central location, exchange your vows, and have your guests toast you to many years of happiness and good luck!

Resources for Casino Theme Wedding

Casino Night Vendors/Suppliers

> > Check out PartyPop's Website at *www.partypop.com*, to find a casino party vendor near you.

> > Visit iParty's Website to find decorations for a casino night theme wedding. *www.iparty.com*

Invitations and Décor

> > Check out Paperworld Invitations (*www.paperworld.invitations.com*), a network of online invitation and gift shop retailers, to create low-cost, creative invitations.

Wine Tasting Theme Wedding

If you are looking for an elegant theme wedding experience that's fun and interactive, consider a wine tasting theme wedding. Similar to a cocktail party, your wine tasting theme wedding would likely be held during the early evening and will provide structured entertainment for your guests.

Step 1. Choose Your Venue.

You have three options for your wine tasting theme wedding venue.

1. You can host the wedding party in a private home.
2. You can locate a local winery to host the wedding party on-site.
3. You can host the wedding party in a function hall.

If you choose the first option, you have a lot of flexibility. Planning a wine-tasting wedding in a private home allows you to hold the event how and when you want. You can select the brands of wine that interest you—or ask your guests to bring a bottle of wine as a wedding present—to keep costs down. Many resources are available to teach you how to host a wine-tasting party, or you can invite a local vintner to host the party for you. Keep in mind that if you choose the latter, you may lose some control over the wine selection and costs, but having an expert lead your theme wedding event can add formality and reduce the pressure on you to plan the perfect wine tasting event.

Another option for your wine tasting theme wedding is to locate a local winery to host your event. Keep in mind that your guest numbers may need to be reduced if you hold a wine tasting wedding at a winery. Many wineries can only accommodate 50 or so people. If you would prefer to have more control over the location and size of your theme wedding, ask your local winery representatives if they will host an event at a location of your choice. Many wineries will host off-site, private parties.

If you decide to hold a wine tasting theme wedding at a function hall, be aware that your choices may be limited. Many venues will not allow you to bring alcohol into the hall. Call around to local hotels and function facilities to see what their alcohol policy is. If your budget allows, you may want to ask a local hotel if it has a sommelier who could host your event at the hotel. You'll probably pay a premium for the wine and the sommelier's services, but you will avoid preparation hassles, such as purchasing wine glasses and accessories.

Step 2. Plan the tasting.

If you and your spouse-to-be are wine connoisseurs who think it would be fun to organize and lead a wine-tasting theme wedding for your guests, here are a few planning tips:

> **Choose your wine type**—Gather a selection of wine by region, date, price, or grape. If you are asking your guests to bring a bottle of wine as a wedding gift, let them know what type of wine you are looking for. (You should try to have fewer than eight wines for your tasting.)

> **Hide the labels**—Most wine tastings are blind, meaning that guests don't know the type of wine they are drinking until all votes are in. Place all wines in a numbered, paper bag, or cover the wine label, to disguise the bottle.

> **Prepare the palate**—Give each guest a wine glass and pour two ounces (1/3 of a glass) of wine per tasting. In between tastings, have guests rinse their glass, and their mouths, with fresh water placed nearby. To personalize your wine tasting wedding, consider purchasing wine glasses etched with your names and wedding date. While costly (you may pay $3 to $10 per glass), personalized wine glasses can distinguish your wine tasting event as a unique wedding celebration.

> **Offer nibblies**—True wine connoisseurs argue that no food should be served until after the tasting, but to keep your guests content, consider serving fancy cheeses, breads, crackers, and fruits.

> **Collect votes**—Ask guests to make notes on the appearance, aroma, and taste of the various wines and discuss as a group which wines they prefer and why.

Resources for a Wine Tasting Theme Wedding

Books

How to Taste: A Guide to Enjoying Wine by Jancis Robinson (New York, NY: Simon & Schuster, 2000). Written by *The Wall Street Journal's* wine enthusiast, this book provides practical and easy-to-understand guidelines for enjoying wine and creating your own wine tasting celebration.

Wine Spectator Complete Wine Tasting Kit, by Harvey Steiman (New York, NY: Wine Spectator Press/M. Shanken Communications, Inc., 2001). This book guides you through the enjoyable process of hosting a wine tasting event, from how to select appropriate wine to what supplies you might need when entertaining your guests to providing the correct instructions for your guests.

Wineries

> Check out the National Association of American Wineries at *www.americanwineries.org/* to locate a winery near you that will host an event.

Wedding Favors and Décor

> ➣ Visit Emily's Specialty Products at *http://esp.logomall.com/* for personalized wine glasses and other customized accessories.

Wine Tasting Techniques

> ➣ Visit Wine Spectator Magazine's Website at *www.winespectator.com* to learn more about hosting a wine tasting theme event.

Mardi Gras Theme Wedding

Nothing spices up February like a good old-fashioned Mardi Gras celebration! If you want a winter wedding that's fun for guests of all ages, consider a Mardi Gras theme.

Step 1. Choose your location.

Mardi Gras parties can be adapted to fit any location, from a city apartment to a sprawling block party. Consider transforming your home into Bourbon Street with lots of colorful decorations—all in purple, green, and gold, the official colors of Mardi Gras. Serve Cajun food to your guests as they listen to the sounds of jazz and zydeco in the background. Colorful party punches, flashing lights, and streamers can transform any space into the French Quarter.

Step 2. Entertain the guests.

Mardi Gras has something for everyone, so it's a great theme for a diverse group of partygoers. Send out Mardi Gras invitations, which you can purchase at most party supply stores along with your decorations. On your invitations, ask your guests to wear purple, green, and gold, and to come prepared for a lively and energetic celebration. If you have a creative group of guests, ask them to make their own masks to bring to the party and reward the most original creations. When your guests arrive, supply them with face paint, feathers, masks (if they didn't bring their own), and lots of colorful beads to create a true carnival atmosphere.

A Mardi Gras theme wedding also provides you with many opportunities for personalization. Party favors, balloons, jester dolls, and hats can be imprinted with your names and wedding date to remind guests of the true reason for your celebration. If lively dancing and an all-you-can-eat buffet of Southern food isn't enough entertainment for your guests, consider some fun party games such as the limbo, Mardi Gras trivia, and best costume prizes. If you have a lot of young children at your theme wedding, you can purchase many age-appropriate games at a local party supply store to keep them occupied.

Step 3. Plan your wedding ceremony.

Most Mardi Gras parties feature crowning a King and a Queen, and therefore are very conducive to a wedding ceremony. Once all of your guests arrive, have your officiant lead a festive wedding ceremony that concludes with you and your new spouse being escorted into the crowd atop a handmade Mardi Gras float!

Mardi Gras Theme Wedding Resources

Invitations

> Visit *www.finestationery.com* for Mardi Gras invitations that you can design and order online.

Mardi Gras Decorations and Party Supplies

> Check out *www.mardisgrasday.com* for decoration ideas and resources.

Unique Wedding Spotlight:
Baseball Theme Wedding

Jim and Mary Assurian knew that a diamond would be a central part of their wedding experience, but it wasn't until after their engagement that they realized just how central a role the diamond would be. Avid baseball fans, Mary and Jim decided to tie the knot in the baseball diamond of their local AAA baseball team, the Hagerstown Suns of Hagerstown, Maryland. "We got engaged at the baseball park. The mascot brought me a dozen pink roses as 'Mary, Will You Marry Me?' flashed in neon lights on the scoreboard. When Jim later suggested getting married at the park, I thought it was a really neat idea," said Mary. If you are interested in a sports theme wedding, you may want to follow Mary and Jim's planning steps.

Step 1. Find and reserve a location.

Two months after their engagement, Jim and Mary spoke with the general manager of the Hagerstown Suns about planning a wedding at the park. Eager to accommodate a fan's unique wedding request, the manager offered information and resources to help the couple plan their special day. "We got the name of the team's baseball supplier and ticket vendor (*www.ticketcraft.com*) and we contacted them to have personalized baseball favors designed for us, as well as wedding invitations that looked like baseball tickets. Instead of seat, row, and section, our wedding 'tickets' said our names, wedding date, and location," said Jim. The team's manager also offered free tickets to the game for the guests, as well as complimentary food and drinks. He even hired a barbershop quartet for the couple's wedding day as a surprise wedding gift.

Baseball Theme Wedding Resources

Many major and minor league baseball parks have function rooms available for rent and many have dedicated event coordinators to help you plan your unique wedding experience. Some of the major league ballparks that are particularly accommodating to theme wedding receptions include:

- Baltimore Orioles (Oriole Park)—*http://baltimore.orioles.mlb.com/*

- Chicago White Sox (U.S. Cellular Field)—*http://chicago.whitesox.mlb.com/*

- Cincinnati Reds (Great American Ballpark)—*http://cincinnati.reds.mlb.com/*

- Colorado Rockies (Coors Field)—*http://colorado.rockies.mlb.com/*

- Detroit Tigers (Comerica Park)—*http://detroit.tigers.mlb.com/*

- Milwaukee Brewers (Miller Park)—*http://milwaukee.brewers.mlb.com/*

- New York Yankees (Yankee Stadium)—*http://newyork.yankees.mlb.com*

- San Francisco Giants (SBC Park)—*http://sanfrancisco.giants.mlb.com/*

Step 2. Select wedding day vendors.

The couple began planning their wedding about six months prior to the wedding day. Once the baseball team's home schedule was finalized, Jim and Mary reserved a reception site at an old mansion several miles from the baseball park. They hired a party bus to chauffeur guests from the park to the reception site, found a caterer and tent rental vendor for the outdoor reception, hired an ordained minister, and worked with the general manager to finalize wedding day details. "It was a lot easier to plan than a traditional wedding," said Jim. "Although you do need to plan for the unanticipated. With this type of unusual wedding, there was a greater potential for things to go wrong, so we really tried to plan well," said Jim.

Step 3. Plan the wedding ceremony.

The wedding guests gathered at the baseball park prior to the team's afternoon game and watched as Mary and Jim walked down an aisle, created by the players' raised bats, dressed in formal wedding attire. They exchanged their vows at home plate and rather than using a ring-bearer to pass their rings, the couple asked the players to get involved. The players taped the rings to a baseball and threw the ball "around the horn" to home plate.

Step 4. Plan the reception.

Following the 15-minute ceremony, the couple and their guests watched half of the game and then filed into the waiting party buses to drive to the reception site. There the guests changed from their casual clothes to more appropriate wedding attire. The reception continued the baseball theme with an ice sculpture of a baseball player, a wedding cake in the shape of a baseball, a rented popcorn machine, and baseball favors—complete with the Hagerstown Suns logo—for the guests. The reception was a relaxed, outdoor affair with games for kids to play and a simple buffet meal.

Step 5. Prepare for guest reactions.

"Everyone who went to the wedding really enjoyed themselves," said Jim when asked about guest reactions to his non-traditional wedding. Some guests embraced the idea more than others. "My family was okay with it. My mom is in the catering business so she's seen a lot of unique weddings and this wasn't too far out of the ordinary," said Jim. "Mary's father was laid back, but her mom had a harder time with it. She is a traditional, very religious woman and I don't think she really took the wedding day seriously."

Despite some mixed reactions to their creative wedding, Jim and Mary would highly encourage other adventurous couples to consider a baseball theme wedding. "Don't let other people try to talk you out of it. Don't let what a few people say count," urges Jim. "If they say that your theme wedding idea is silly or you should do something more traditional, don't let it prevent you from doing what you want to do. This is your day and you should enjoy it the way you want to. Plan something that you think will be fun, and your guests will enjoy it because, ultimately, they are there to support you on your wedding day."

$ Jim and Mary's Baseball Theme Wedding Details $	
Personalized "baseball ticket" Invitations	= $312 ($1.25 x 250)
Personalized baseball favors baseball x 300 baseballs)	= $450 ($1.50/
Officiant	= $100 charitable donation in lieu of payment
Party bus to reception site	= $1,000
Tuxedo rental	= $100
Wedding gown	= $100
Ballpark rental/ceremony	= Free
Guest game-day tickets and refreshments	= Free
Barbershop quartet	= Free
Total baseball park theme wedding costs	= $2,062
Total planning time	= 6 Months
Total guests	= 200

Unique Wedding Spotlight: Murder Mystery Theme Wedding

Amanda Trombley and Heiko Glessmenn knew that a traditional wedding wasn't right for them. Cofounders of a

Web development and marketing company, they wanted a stress-free wedding celebration that would involve their guests, allow everyone to have a great time, and center on friends and family more than bride and groom. Most of all, they didn't want their guests to be bored! Here are the steps they took to plan their Murder Mystery Theme Wedding.

1. Select your theme.

As they contemplated various non-traditional wedding options, Amanda and Heiko knew that they wanted to plan a wedding that would be special for both of them rather than having it just be the "bride's day." "It's the groom's day too," says Amanda, "and if you don't include him it can set a bad precedent for the rest of the marriage." Together, they brainstormed various wedding options, and both became very excited by the prospect of a Murder Mystery Theme Wedding. This unique wedding idea would surely include all guests, provide lots of laughs, and blend ceremony with entertainment.

2. Contact wedding vendors.

Heiko and Amanda wanted to get married near the ocean and began scoping out wedding sites that could accommodate a theme wedding with 50 guests. The couple quickly realized that mention of the word "wedding" tripled event costs, so they started referring to their celebration as a "family reunion" when interacting with vendors. "I felt a little uptight about it because I am usually an honest person, but it made sense to do it," says Amanda. This new strategy enabled the couple to find the perfect wedding venue. Working with a local Realtor to find a weeklong rental property for the "reunion," they booked a sprawling, oceanfront mansion near Newport, Rhode Island, that would cost only $1,900 for the week.

In addition to disguising their wedding, the couple also took some creative steps when purchasing other wedding products. After visiting a floral shop that wanted $500 for a bouquet, Amanda and Heiko discovered a farm stand near their wedding mansion that would provide 100 fresh-picked flowers for only $40. After visiting a cake shop that demanded $2,000 for a wedding cake, Amanda and Heiko found a local ice cream shop in Rhode Island that would produce an elegant cake for $225. And after being disgusted at the exorbitant prices for traditional wedding dresses, Amanda visited a dressmaker in Chinatown and had an authentic Asian wedding dress made especially for her at a price of only $200.

3. Find a murder mystery company.

Now that the wedding location was set, their wedding date confirmed, and a justice of the peace prepared to marry them, the couple wanted to focus on the entertainment portion of their wedding celebration. They called around to several corporate event planning companies that advertised murder mystery parties and finally found one that would service their unique wedding for only $1,000.

Open to new opportunities and eager to fulfill the couple's unique wedding day wishes, the murder mystery company planned an extraordinary wedding event. They met with Amanda and Heiko prior to their wedding day to hear how the couple's wedding would be organized and to learn about the subtle idiosyncrasies of the guests. Then, as guests arrived for the wedding celebration, the theatre company took more mental notes of the guests and had the couple identify various friends and family members so that the actors could incorporate them into the action. The result was an interactive, side-splitting party that guests continue to reminisce about.

4. Invite guests.

Several weeks prior to their wedding, Amanda and Heiko sent out informal wedding invitations to their 50 guests. After sending their wedding invitations, Amanda and Heiko began getting calls from guests confused about what they should wear and how they should act at the wedding. "People just aren't accustomed to a wedding that doesn't follow traditional protocol. They aren't sure what to do," says Amanda. Heiko and Amanda reassured their guests by asking that they dress comfortably and casually and enjoy the murder mystery entertainment. They explained that the wedding would not have traditional customs, but would be entirely original and fun for all.

Originally perplexed by the couple's non-traditional wedding plans, friends and family members grew excited about the unique wedding. Close family members were invited to spend the week with the couple at the mansion, including Heiko's grandmother, who traveled from Germany for the first time to the United States. Renting the wedding venue for the week contributed to a relaxing, family-oriented wedding celebration. "The family really wasn't included in the wedding planning until this point, so they were happy to be involved and spend time with us at the mansion," says Amanda.

5. Attend to last-minute details.

To keep costs down and ensure a tailor-made wedding, Heiko and Amanda handled most of the last-minute wedding details themselves, including putting together the flower arrangements only three hours before their ceremony! While they did hire a caterer, they purchased most of their party supplies and decorations from stores such as the Christmas Tree Shoppe. In the end, their personal touches and collaborative approach created a simple, civil ceremony followed by a hilarious celebration that focused on family and fun.

For less than $8,000, Heiko and Amanda planned and executed a week-long wedding celebration and murder mystery theme party that included an oceanfront mansion, photographer, caterer, cake, flowers, party supplies, entertainment, guest accommodations, wedding attire, and an elegant ceremony.

Tips for Other Theme Wedding Couples

1. **Avoid the word "wedding" when planning a theme wedding party and save thousands of dollars!**

2. **If family and friends are important to your wedding, find ways to prolong the wedding celebration beyond a four-hour party.**

3. **Be creative when selecting wedding decorations and supplies.** Contact local shops and other vendors who don't typically cater to weddings to find great deals and excellent service.

Murder Mystery Theme Wedding Resources

> **Bed and Breakfast Inns Online**—Many bed-and-breakfast inns offer murder mystery parties and can accommodate wedding groups. Check out *www.bbonline.com/murder.html* for a location near you.

> **Board Game Central**—Choose from several murder mystery board game options to host your own murder mystery party. *www.boardgamecentral.com*

> **CyberRentals**—View thousands of vacation rental listings to find a property at which to host a murder mystery theme wedding. *www.cyberrentals.com*

> **Dinner and a Murder**—Offers a variety of downloadable murder mystery games suitable for all types of audiences.
>
> *www.dinnerandamurder.com*

> **Invitation to Murder**—Hosts on-site murder mystery parties nationwide.
>
> *www.invitationtomurder.com*

> **Killing Time**—True "murder consultants," this acting group offers several murder mystery plots to fit your unique wedding.
>
> *www.killingtime.com*

> **Murder Mystery Players**—A comedy theatre company that conducts interactive murder mystery weddings. *www.mysteryplayers.com*

Chapter 9

Adventure Weddings

If the wedding ideas presented up to now still seem too conventional for you, then this chapter will help you to plan the extreme wedding you are dreaming about. An adventure wedding is often centered around a favorite hobby or sport. It may take place by land, sea, or air. It could be close to home or in a far-off land. It could involve just the two of you or a cadre of friends and family members. Adventure weddings require a great deal of creativity and collaboration, but if you and your partner long for a wedding that would never make it to the pages of *Elegant Bride*, then here are some planning steps for you to consider.

As the marketplace for non-traditional weddings expands, adventure weddings have become increasingly popular. Couples who plan an adventure wedding, sometimes called an extreme wedding, are inventive, independent-minded people who love the outdoors, enjoy setting new trends, and are not afraid to take risks. They often begin their wedding planning by contemplating a destination wedding or elopement, but imagine a wedding experience that is more fun and pioneering.

You may want to plan an adventure wedding if:

> You are searching for an extraordinary wedding experience.

> You are a risk-taker and don't need to be in control of each wedding detail.

> You like excitement.

> You have a lot of hobbies.

> You want a wedding that is connected to your interests.

> You want your guests to have fun.

> You like the idea of a destination wedding—with a little something extra!

> You want to save money.

> You are creative and can think "outside the box" to plan an original wedding.

> You want to combine an exhilarating ceremony with a post-wedding celebration.

Are You Up for an Adventure?

Adventure weddings are daring and certainly not for everyone. They can require a lot of preparation and inspiration and will likely cause some family members and friends to wonder if you have lost your mind. You and your partner will need to decide together if you can tolerate the risks associated with an adventure wedding—both physical and emotional! To see if an adventure wedding is right for you, take a look at the Adventure Preference Quiz.

Adventure Preference Quiz

I would prefer to read:

__ *Outdoor Life*

__ *Better Homes and Gardens*

I would prefer to shop at:
__ L.L. Bean.
__ Macy's.

I would prefer to:
__ hike a mountain .
__ lay on the beach.

I would prefer to:
__ jump off a cliff.
__ watch others jump off a cliff.

I would prefer to drive:
__ a Hummer.
__ a Toyota Camry.

I would prefer to:
__ compete in a triathlon.
__ go for a walk.

Did you find yourself drawn to the adventurous activities, or did you prefer to be an onlooker? Do you prefer the rugged outdoors more than domestic pursuits? If you have an adventurous spirit and are not afraid to get your hands dirty, then dive right into an adventure wedding. You are the type of couple that thrives on excitement and challenge. In fact, you probably spend much of your free time enjoying outdoor events or trying new things. An adventure wedding is a natural endeavor for you, and you should feel comfortable taking it on. Still, in the interest of full disclosure, you should consider the pros and cons of an adventure wedding before plunging into the planning stages:

Adventure Wedding Trade-Offs

Pros	Cons
They can be exciting and fun.	They can cause family revolts.
They can be tailored to your interests.	They can take a lot of time to plan.
They can be enjoyable for guests.	They call for some imagination.
They can be planned as a couple.	They can be costly.
They can be combined with other unique wedding options (such as destination weddings).	They require an easygoing outlook. (Not ideal for control-freaks!)
There are many options and vendors available.	They can be risky.

Choose Your Adventure

If you are one of those couples looking to say I do"with a big twist, and the drawbacks of an adventure wedding are insignificant to you, then start planning. Your first planning step is to decide on the type of adventure wedding that suits you. Some couples choose their wedding adventures based on similar sporting interests or memories of first dates. If you and your partner met while bungee-jumping, then why not tie the knot propelling off a bridge? Other couples are open to anything exciting and are looking for ideas. To help you narrow down your choices and select your ideal wedding adventure, you and your partner should take the A-to-Z Adventure Questionnaire.

The questionnaire highlights many exciting adventures for you and your partner to think about. Select the activities that you both enjoy the most and start investigating wedding possibilities. You could get married on the top of a ski slope. You could take a safari to Africa. You could hike the Grand Canyon. You could take an Alaskan wilderness cruise. The options are endless!

Some wedding adventures can take a bit of time to plan, and other adventures can be spontaneous. Once you and your partner narrow down your list of possible options, then decide how much time, effort, and expense each one would involve. If you decide to stage a "wedding kidnap" adventure to Bali, as described in Michael and Mindi's adventure wedding (p. 229), then start planning early to book flights, reserve hotel rooms, notify employers, and comply with exotic travel and marriage requirements. If you decide to get married underwater while on a trip to the Caribbean, then you probably only need a day or two to get scuba certified!

While adventure wedding couples like to take risks, you may want to resist tackling a new sport or activity on your wedding day. If you have never before gone spelunking, it may not be a good idea to try it out on your wedding day. If you would like to experiment with a new hobby, make a first attempt prior to your wedding just to make sure it is something you want to commemorate forever.

A-to-Z Adventure Questionnaire

Which of the following activities do you enjoy? (Check all that apply)

___ Airplane flying	___ Caving
___ Backpacking	___ Cycling
___ Ballooning	___ Desert backpacking
___ Bird-watching	___ Dogsledding
___ Bungee-jumping	___ Downhill skiing
___ Camping	___ Exotic travel
___ Canoeing	___ Fencing

__ Fishing   __ Jogging
__ Glacier mountaineering __ Judo
__ Helicopter sight-seeing __ Kayaking
__ Hiking   __ Luge
__ Horseback riding   __ Mountain biking
__ Ice climbing   __ Mountain climbing
__ In-line skating   __ NASCAR racing
__ Orienteering   __ Snorkeling
__ Paintball   __ Surfing
__ Parachuting   __ Tenting
__ Parasailing   __ Triathlons
__ Quail hunting   __ Underwater sports
__ River rafting   __ Volcano hiking
__ Rock climbing   __ Waterskiing
__ Sailing   __ Wilderness expeditions
__ Scuba diving   __ Winter camping
__ Skydiving   __ Whitewater rafting
__ Snowboarding   __ X-Country Skiing
__ Snowmobiling   __ Yoga
__ Snowshoeing   __ Zebra watching

Adventure Wedding Ideas

Let's suppose you and your partner checked several of the activities featured in the Adventure Wedding Questionnaire and you have a few months to plan your wedding. You have the ability to coordinate a wedding adventure around any of these activities. If you are both avid NASCAR fans, plan a racing adventure wedding at the Kentucky Speedway (*www.kentuckyspeedway.com*). If you are volcano enthusiasts, get married at the Hawaii Volcanoes National Park (*www.nps.gov/havo*). Once you commit to planning a wedding adventure around your varied interests and passions, you open yourself to many exciting wedding options.

Combine an adventure wedding with a destination wedding, a theme wedding, or elopement, or plan an entirely unique wedding adventure. If you do want to bring along guests, however, be aware that you may be more limited in your adventure wedding options. Even if they love you deeply, your family members may not be willing to jump out of a plane or ascend a cliff to see you tie the knot. If having guests at your wedding is a priority, then select a wedding adventure that requires a low or moderate skill-level to keep everyone safe and comfortable.

This chapter gets you started on your adventure wedding planning by providing suggestions for designing four popular types of wedding adventures: a wilderness expedition through an adventure travel company, a slope-side wedding, an African safari wedding, and a skydiving wedding. You will also hear how two couples planned real-life adventure weddings, including a "wedding kidnap" and an underwater wedding.

Prearranged Travel Expeditions

Perhaps you would like to plan a wilderness trek that doesn't require a lot of time-consuming effort on your end and that you know will be safe and high-quality. Maybe you and your partner love hiking, backpacking, and kayaking and would enjoy creating a wedding adventure around these interests. Consider teaming up with a company that specializes in wilderness adventures, such as Outward Bound or REI Adventures. These groups allow you to choose a trip around your varied interests. Outward Bound (*www.outwardbound.com*) can accommodate couples who are looking for exciting outdoor excursions that focus on renewal and trust-building. If you would like to combine your adventure wedding with a destination wedding for your family, consider REI Adventures (*www.rei.com/adventures*) or another adventure travel program available through your local travel agent. Adventure trips could range from backpacking across the Rockies to hiking in the mountains of Tibet. And the best part is that you can sign up for these trips online and feel secure that your trip will be led by an experienced guide.

Planning Tips

While they offer a variety of outdoor excursions of different lengths and skill level, prearranged wilderness treks offered by adventure travel companies have their drawbacks. First, most don't cater to weddings, so you will need to be creative when it comes to your ceremony. For example, you could plan a small ceremony at the base of the mountain just prior to your expedition. Or, if your trip's itinerary allows for exploration breaks, you could get married in one of the local spots on your trek. If you are thinking about a wilderness excursion through an adventure travel company, realize that the focus will be much more on the adventure than the wedding. You will need to work your ceremony around the trip's established agenda, which could get frustrating.

Another potential drawback to a prearranged adventure travel wedding is the cost. A seven-day Outward Bound backpacking trip in Colorado, for example, will cost about $1,300 per person, and a seven-day REI Adventures sea kayaking tour in Vancouver would cost about the same. And you often have to purchase new, expensive gear that could thrust you into the red. Still, if you compare these costs to a traditional wedding, you will be spending far less for your unique celebration.

Finally, a third drawback could be planning time. Some prearranged adventure travel trips can sell out up to six months in advance, so start exploring your options early.

Adventure Travel Resources

> ➤ America Outdoors—International association representing adventure travel outfitters, tour companies and outdoor educators. *www.americaoutdoors.org*

> ➤ Away.com—Online network of adventure travel resources and organizations. *www.away.com*

> ➤ Eco-Travel Magazine—An online resource that offers information on eco-tours and nature excursions, including a searchable directory of eco-travel providers. *www.ecotravel.com*

> ➤ iExplore—Funded by National Geographic, iExplore helps you research and reserve off-the-beaten-path travel adventures. *www.iexplore.com*

Slopeside Wedding

Maybe you don't want to be tied down to the whims of an adventure travel company and would like to create your own adventure. There are many vendors that specialize in adventure weddings that match your interests. Identify your interests and start searching for people who can help you plan your perfect day.

If you and your partner are avid skiers or snowboarders, for example, why not consider a slopeside wedding? Most major ski resorts can accommodate mountaintop weddings and many even cater to them. At Colorado's Vail Mountain Resort (*www.vail.snow.com*), for example, you could plan a simple mountaintop wedding dressed in your snow gear followed by an elaborate wedding reception. Or you and your partner could retreat to your private chalet. If the ceremony is more important to you, you could choose an elegant ceremony in a specially designed amphitheater overlooking the mountains, and then celebrate on the slopes.

Annual Loveland Mountaintop Wedding

If you are looking for a truly wild slopeside wedding, you and your partner should join the over 100 couples who marry each Valentine's Day at the Annual Loveland Mountaintop Wedding at the Loveland Ski Area in Georgetown, Colorado.

A mass ceremony is performed at the top of the mountain and all couples and guests then ski or snowboard to the lodge. (All participants must be capable of getting down the hill.) The ceremony is followed by a reception with food, spirits and prizes.

Cost:

> Brides and grooms can take advantage of a 2-for-1 lift ticket deal (less than $50), and free admission to the reception.

> Guests must purchase their own lift tickets and pay $10 each to attend the reception.

For more information, visit *www.skiloveland.com*.

Planning Tips

Most major ski resorts have their own function coordinators who plan weddings and provide information about facilities and services on their Websites. These function coordinators can be tremendous resources for you, particularly if you find someone who is supportive of your adventure wedding. Look around—they're out there! Be warned, however, that most ski resorts, and their function coordinators, cater to traditional brides and grooms who will be spending thousands of dollars to get married with the scenic backdrop of a ski slope. Unless it's what you are looking for, try not to get drafted into planning just another traditional wedding at a ski resort. Be persistent when contacting ski resort function managers. Tell them specifically what you are looking for and ask if they can provide you with assistance.

If you will be staying in resort-affiliated lodging, and are looking for help in identifying an officiant to marry you atop the mountain, tell the function coordinator what you are planning and ask for a referral for an officiant. Ask if they have other resources to help you, but be firm in your wedding wishes. If you have found an officiant on your own who will marry you privately on the mountain without any attention from the resort, but you would like to have a reception for family members and friends, you may choose not to tell the function coordinator you are planning a wedding reception. Often they have pre-set menus and pricing plans for "wedding receptions." Explain that you are hosting a family party and ask what spaces they have available to accommodate you.

Also be aware that some ski resorts can only accommodate your "slopeside" wedding in the summer! If you are looking for a winter wedding, you may need to be creative and find your own wedding officiant—or ask the function coordinator for a referral—and secretly set up your mountaintop wedding.

Slopeside Wedding Resources

> **Ski magazine**—The magazine for ski aficionados. *www.skimag.com*

> **Lake Tahoe Weddings**—Online resource for getting married in the Lake Tahoe ski resort. *www.tahoesbest.com/Weddings*

> **Steamboat USA**—Information about getting married in this Colorado ski town. *www.steamboat.com*

> **Whistler Ski Resort**—Information on planning a wedding at the Whistler Ski Resort in Vancouver, British Columbia. *www.whistler.com*

> **Wildcat Mountain**—Wildcat Mountain in Pinkham Notch, New Hampshire specializes in unique, personalized ski adventure weddings. *www.skiwildcat.com/weddings.html*

African Safari Adventure Wedding

If you checked off "zebra watching" as one of your favorite pastimes, how about considering an African safari adventure wedding? The range of African safari options is enormous, from rustic, camp-like excursions to 5-star luxury accommodations. Observe exotic animals. Hike the Serengeti Plain. Learn about Africa's diverse culture and rich history. Similar to the pre-arranged travel trips described earlier, there are many adventure travel organizations that focus exclusively on African safari trips.

Planning Tips

Check out *www.gorptravel.com* for an assortment of safari options geared towards couples or families. Trips are offered year-round, so you can choose an adventure that fits in with your wedding timeline, and the favorable currency exchange rate means that you get a lot for your money. Still, prices are hefty. An eight-day trek in Tanzania, with luxury accommodations, starts at $3,000 per person plus airfare and medical insurance. Or customize a trip to Botswana and Zimbabwe for just the two of you or with your family members. Select a departure date that works for you, and visit the most remote areas of Africa while enjoying great dining and lodging. A 13-day, customized trek through Gorp starts at $5,000 per person plus airfare and medical insurance.

As for the ceremony, again you may need to be creative. If you choose a customized safari through a travel organization such as Gorp, then trip consultants can work with you to schedule time for your ceremony. A prearranged trip might require more effort on your part to find time before, during, or after the trek to exchange your vows.

If you are looking for complete freedom when planning your African safari adventure wedding, then consider working with a resort at your destination of choice. Adventure weddings in Africa are becoming very popular as couples look to say I do in places other than sandy beaches. Many African hotels and resorts cater specifically to weddings for international visitors and have an assortment of packages for you to choose from. These resorts would also be able to help you through some of the legal requirements associated with marrying in Africa.

For a romantic wedding in the African bush, you may want to consider Ngala Tented Safari Camp. Located within South Africa's Kruger National Park, you can watch antelope walk by as you enjoy the pleasantries of a five-star resort. The resort specializes in designing safari weddings and will work with you to select a ceremony location and theme that appeals to you. Wedding packages, which begin at $1,000 plus lodging, can include ceremony, dinner, entertainment, flowers, champagne in the bush, and your own personal Land Rover! Check out *http://honeymoon.safari.co.za/* for more information on Ngala weddings and other resources.

If an inclusive wedding package in the wilderness of Tanzania is more to your liking, then consider exchanging vows at the Ngorongoro Crater Lodge (*www.ngorongorocrater.com*). You will be led to your rose-petal laden ceremony to the sounds of traditional African drum music and chanting and then enjoy champagne to the sounds of the wild. You and your guests will be treated to luxury accommodations, complete with a private butler who will satisfy your every whim! All inclusive room rates, including daily safari trips and meals, begin at $445 per person, per night.

Some African countries are easier to get married in than others, so you may want to consider the legal requirements when selecting your safari destination. Getting married in South Africa, Morroco, or Tanzania, for example, is fairly straightforward. They welcome foreign nationals and do not require residency or blood tests. All you need are valid passports, birth certificates, and proof of divorce/death, if applicable. For other countries, such as Kenya, the process is a bit more complex with the added requirement of a statutory declaration stating that you are free to marry. Your vital records will typically need to be translated up to six weeks prior to your wedding.

It is a good idea to book your safari with an adventure travel company or a resort that specializes in weddings. They will share with you the legal requirements, identify a qualified officiant, and make certain that all preparations are taken care of prior to your arrival.

Africa Safari Wedding Resources

> *Travel Africa* **Magazine**—Quarterly magazine on Africa travel and news.
  www.travelafricamag.com

> **Africa Guide**—An online resource providing information on all African countries, travel and tourism, customs and people.
  www.africaguide.com

> **African News Online**—Provides up-to-date news and information on Africa from more than 60 international news sources. *www.africanews.org*

> **CC Africa**—Safari company specializing in adventure weddings and honeymoons.
  www.afroventures.com/

> **Cedarberg Travel**—A travel agency that coordinates personalized African safari weddings and adventures. *www.cedarberg-travel.com*

> **Carr-Hartley Safariland**—High-end safari operators that create tailor-made African safari adventures. *www.carrhartley.com*

Mid-Air Matrimony

You are certain that an adventure wedding is right for you, but you are looking for something truly outrageous. For couples seeking exhilarating, death-defying nuptials, consider a wedding in mid-air.

Skydiving weddings are gaining popularity and so are the resources to help couples plan this unique wedding option. Most skydiving companies allow you to marry on the plane and seal your ceremony with a kiss as you jump into your new life together. Some even have wedding officiants on staff who will take the plunge with you—just make sure that you hold onto your wedding bands! And many full-service skydiving companies will accommodate a family affair, allowing groups of up to 16 people to jump together to celebrate your union. If not everyone is eager to jump with you, many established skydiving companies have landing facilities that can accommodate observers and offer function rental facilities.

Planning Tips

As with planning any wedding, there are benefits and drawbacks to a skydiving wedding. One of the great benefits of a skydiving wedding is that rates are reasonable (typically costing $150 per person for novice jumpers) and diving packages often include a videotape of your jump (taken by your guide) and photography. These add-ons typically cost less than $100 and provide a great way to commemorate your unique wedding.

Another benefit is that you don't need to be an experienced skydiver to enjoy a mid-air wedding. Most skydiving programs involve at least an hour of ground training and are led by experienced jumpers who join you on your descent to ensure everything goes fine.

A third benefit of a skydiving wedding is ease of planning and scheduling. If you can find an available officiant, you could get married on-the-spot with little planning required. Many skydiving companies allow walk-ins based on availability and should be able to accommodate your unique wedding request. Try to find a vendor that has experience with mid-air weddings—or at least engagements—so that the process will go more smoothly.

There are some drawbacks to planning a skydiving wedding that you should know. First, weather can be a factor. If there are high winds or inclement weather, your wedding may need to be postponed. This could be a setback if you have rented out a function facility, have invited guests to witness your wedding, or need to reschedule with your officiant.

Another possible drawback is jumper restrictions. Most reputable skydiving companies require all jumpers to be at least 18 years old, weigh less than 240 pounds, and be in good physical (and mental) health.

The final obvious drawback is fear of injury or death. While few people get seriously injured from a skydive, anything is possible when jumping out of an airplane at several thousand feet. You would hate to begin your life together with you or your loved ones in the emergency room with twisted ankles or broken legs, so be aware of the risks before "jumping" into this exciting wedding adventure.

Skydiving Wedding Resources

➢ **United States Parachute Association (USPA)—** Professional association of skydiving and parachuting companies. Make certain that your vendor is a member of this organization when reserving your wedding jump. This site provides a searchable database to help you find a member company in your area. *www.uspa.org*

> ➢ **Dropzone.com**—An online resource for skydivers around the world, this site offers news and information on skydiving, including a database of skydiving vendors by state and country. *www.dropzone.com*

> ➢ *Skydiving* **Magazine**—The magazine for skydiving and parachuting enthusiasts. Visit their Website for answers to frequently asked questions about skydiving or to order a subscription. *www.skydivingmagazine.com*

Unique Wedding Spotlight: Kidnap Wedding

It was 4 o'clock in the morning when someone rustled Mindi Ramsey from her sleep, ordered her into the car, and drove away. There was no warning, nothing to make her suspect that she would be snatched so unexpectedly on that fall morning in 1999. Sounds like a horrible kidnapping, right? You may be wondering why you didn't hear about it on primetime news.

Mindi's kidnapping wasn't flashed on the front page of any newspapers. In fact, few have heard about her ordeal until now. Mindi was the target of a wedding kidnap. The assailant? Her boyfriend, Michael.

Michael chose to follow wedding tradition when he planned to kidnap his bride and marry her in a faraway land. In medieval times, wedding kidnaps occurred quite frequently when a warrior would steal a bride from her clan and bring along his "best man" to fight off anyone trying to stop the groom in his crime. The warrior and his kidnapped bride would then take a month-long honeymoon that involved feeding the bride a concoction of honey and mead to keep her in a prolonged state of drunkenness. If you would like to plan a "traditional" wedding kidnap with a modern-day twist, then read how Michael's creative plotting led to a wedding day adventure the couple continues to cherish.

Step 1. Select your victim.

A year prior to the kidnapping, Michael started plotting his crime. He and Mindi had been together for nine years and they knew that someday they would get engaged and marry. Michael realized early on that he wanted a unique wedding and decided that Bali would be the perfect location for him and Mindi to tie the knot.

He found his "best man" accomplice—his college roommate who was originally from Indonesia, home of Bali. Together, the duo secretly planned the wedding kidnap for the following September 1999.

Step 2. Scope out the crime scene.

With the help of his accomplice, Michael began to finalize details for his adventure wedding. His former roommate contacted a hotel in Bali that specializes in weddings. The hotel's function coordinator was able to handle all wedding day details, including reserving a nearby, authentic Buddhist temple for the ceremony, selecting an officiant, hiring a photographer, and ordering indigenous hibiscus leaves for the ceremony.

As for flights, Michael had the great fortune of working for an airline and was able to reserve complimentary, stand-by tickets to Bali. Flying stand-by could cause some confusion and stress, given the number of connections and uncertainty in flight patterns, but Michael was willing to take his chances. This was an adventure wedding, right? He had to assume some risks.

Step 3. Gather necessary booty.

While the hotel in Bali was able to handle most of the travel and wedding day details, Michael did have some tasks to perform at home. The hotel informed Michael of the legal requirements for getting married in Bali. Two of the primary requirements were copies of an original birth certificate for both the bride and groom, and a black-and-white photo of the couple for the wedding certificate.

Michael had hit a snare. How was he going to ask Mindi (or her parents) for an original birth certificate, and get black and white photos taken, without generating suspicion? He lied. Several months prior to their wedding day, Michael told Mindi he thought the couple should have all of their vital records in one place, so he asked Mindi to have her mother mail her a birth certificate. She didn't seem doubtful of his intentions, so Michael moved on to Bali wedding requirement number two. He picked just the right moment one evening as the couple was cheerful and joking to bring out a roll of black-and-white film and started taking photos. Again, no suspicion.

Step 4. Notify innocent bystanders.

While the wedding kidnap was secretly planned and Michael did not want friends and family members to be aware of the wedding until after it took place, there were some people who needed to be informed of the nine-day trek to Bali. A couple of months prior to the wedding, Michael contacted Mindi's employer, told him that he was surprising Mindi with a tropical vacation, and scheduled time off for her. He called his employer and did the same.

Step 5. Execute the kidnapping.

Early in the morning, Michael woke Mindi and told her that they were going on an adventure. He led her to the car, which he had already packed with bags for the two of them, and drove to the airport. He wouldn't tell Mindi where their flight was headed.

Mindi, a good sport with a spontaneous spirit, was open to a jet-setting adventure. Although Michael had done a great job at notifying Mindi's employer about the trip, there were other job-related appointments that Mindi, a journal-ist, needed to reschedule. After a few phone calls, Mindi was ready for anything Michael had planned, but a wed-ding in Bali was the furthest thing from her mind.

Step 6. Go in for the kill.

Luckily, Mindi and Michael made all of their necessary flight connections and were on their way from California to Bali. Mindi still had no idea what was going on and thought Michael just wanted to surprise her with a fun getaway. But as the plane reached altitude over the Pacific Ocean, Michael unbuckled his seatbelt, kneeled down in front of Mindi, and asked her to marry him. In one hand, he held a diamond engagement ring and in the other, a guidebook for Bali. As the couple celebrated their engagement, Michael then told Mindi of his remaining plans. The wedding cer-emony was to be held two days after their arrival in Bali. Not eager for a traditional wedding, Mindi was thrilled with the news of their impending nuptials and in awe of Michael's creativity and skillful planning.

Step 7. Celebrate your victory.

After arriving at the hotel in Bali, Michael and Mindi went sightseeing, enjoyed the tropical weather, and shopped for their wedding day attire. Mindi found a handmade, Indonesian-laced dress, and Michael purchased a tropical shirt.

On the day of their wedding, they visited the Buddhist temple in which they would be married. Both spiritual people without strong ties to an organized religion, Michael and Mindi enjoyed the idea of a Buddhist ceremony that would reinforce love and tolerance. The ceremony was conducted in both Sanscrit and English, and the couple was wrapped in a traditional yellow silk cloth to symbolize their union. "It was the most romantic thing anyone had ever done for me," said Mindi of her wedding adventure. "It was my dream wedding on the most beautiful place on earth."

Following their wedding ceremony, Mindi and Michael enjoyed a traditional Balian "reception" dinner of cow brains—adding to the uniqueness of this adventure wedding. The remaining days of their wedding kidnap were spent traveling through the countryside, exploring their tropical paradise. "We tried to spend money," said Mindi, "but everything in Bali was so cheap." The couple's week long adventure wedding, including hotels, food and clothing, cost less than $1,000.

Step 8. Prepare to be caught.

When they returned home, Michael and Mindi had wedding announcements printed to inform friends and family of their marriage. Most of their loved ones were elated, but Mindi's mother was slightly disappointed.

To please her mother, Mindi and Michael allowed mom to plan a traditional wedding reception for 150 friends and family members. "It didn't bother me," said Mindi of her mother's plans. "A traditional wedding ends up not being a day for you, but for everyone else. We just wanted to make sure that we had our day first."

Tips for Other Adventure Wedding Couples

1. Plan the wedding you want. The most important thing is to plan the wedding that you want. For some people, that means making their parents happy, but for many others it involves planning a wedding for just the two of you. The opportunities for an adventure wedding are endless— all you have to do is go for it!

2. Start planning early to ensure a successful kidnapping.

3. Be certain that your partner will be receptive to a wedding kidnap. You don't want the marriage to be over before it starts!

$ Mindi and Michael's Bali Adventure Wedding Details $

Hotel (including temple, officiant, and photographer)	= $500
Wedding day couples massage	= $10
Bride's dress	= $50
Bride's shoes	= $30
Groom's attire (tropical shirt and trousers)	= $60
Car rental	= $100
Wedding night dinner and bridal suite	= $60
Total wedding costs	= $910
Total planning time	= 12 Months

Bali Adventure Wedding Resources

> ➤ **Bali Tourism Authority**—Provides information and resources on Bali history, customs, and tourism. *www.balitourismauthority.net*

> ➤ **Indonesia Tourism**—Information on traveling to Indonesia. *www.tourismindonesia.com*

> ➤ **Bali Weddings**—A wedding planning company specializing in unique Bali weddings for foreigners, this Website provides helpful information on the legal requirements for marrying in Bali, as well as ideas for various wedding options. *www.baliweddings.com*

> ➤ **Fodors.com**—International travel site that provides information on Bali attractions, climate, accommodations, and culture. *www.fodors.com*

> ➤ **U.S. Department of State**—The State Department issues travel warnings to many parts of the world in which American tourists may not be welcome. Since the Bali tourist bombing of 2002, Americans are dissuaded from visiting

Indonesia. For updated travel information and advisories, visit: *http://travel.state.gov/ indonesia.html*.

Unique Wedding Spotlight: Underwater Adventure Wedding

The number of adventurous couples choosing underwater weddings is quickly growing. In September 2003, 105 divers in St. Croix, Virgin Islands, broke the previous Guinness Book of World Records benchmark for the largest underwater wedding! Submerged 10 feet into the ocean waters, the bride and groom exchanged their vows in front of a minister and more than 100 guests.

In March of 1996, Leanne Miller and Otto Rutten chose to combine their love of the sea with their love for each other and plan an underwater adventure wedding. Both marine biologists, the couple lived and worked in the Florida Keys. As part of their work, they were actively involved with the National Undersea Research Program's Aquarius undersea habitat. Like the International Space Station, Aquarius is a self-functioning scientific laboratory that is located three-and-a-half miles offshore at a depth of 60 feet. Abutting some of the world's most remarkable coral reefs, scientists live and work in Aquarius on multi-day missions to research ocean environments.

Early in their engagement, Leanne and Otto discussed getting married on, near, or under the ocean. Then one day, a colleague suggested that the couple get married in Aquarius! By selecting a wedding venue linked to their interests and the interests of their friends and colleagues, Leanne and Otto were able to easily plan their underwater wedding. While the Aquarius is off-limits to non-NOAA researchers, the steps that Leanne and Otto took to plan their adventure wedding are worthwhile for other underwater brides and grooms.

3 Months Prior to Underwater Wedding Day

> **Select wedding date.** Three months prior to their wedding day, Leanne and Otto scheduled a time for a brief ceremony to take place amongst their normal workplace activities at Aquarius. A close colleague of the couple offered to become licensed as a notary public so that he could officiate the underwater ceremony.

> **Purchase wedding bands and décor.** Continuing to tie their nautical interests with their adventure wedding, Leanne and Otto traveled to Key West to purchase dolphin-engraved gold wedding bands and they selected an oceanic sculpture from Wyland Galleries (*www.wylandgalleries.com*) to adorn their wedding cake.

> **Make reservations.** After selecting their wedding date and purchasing wedding bands and decorations, the adventurous couple obtained a marriage license and booked a honeymoon getaway to follow their underwater wedding.

2 Months Prior to Underwater Wedding Day

> **Select wedding party.** Fortunately for Leanne and Otto, most of their close friends were also their colleagues who worked on the Aquarius and who offered to assume various wedding roles. Two months prior to the wedding, Leanne and Otto asked four colleagues to serve as best man, maid of honor, videographer and photographer.

1 Month Prior to Underwater Wedding Day

> **Send out reception invitations.** Unfortunately, specialized training requirements and workplace regulations prevented any guests from attending the Aquarius ceremony, but the couple

sent out invitations one month prior to their wedding date asking friends and family to attend a post-wedding celebration in Key Largo following the ceremony. Another generous colleague and his wife offered use of their home for the wedding reception.

The Wedding Day

> **Finalize reception details.** On their wedding day, Leanne and Otto spent a couple of hours in the morning purchasing food and drinks, and picking up a cake for their post-wedding celebration.

> **Embark!** In the early afternoon, the couple departed by boat to Aquarius. Friends, coworkers, and the parents of the bride were present to bid "bon voyage" to the wedding cruise.

> **Prepare for the unexpected.** "The seas were quite rough, as they tend to be in the springtime, so by the time we reached Aquarius, our photographer was seasick," said Leanne, of one minor wedding day setback. The photographer stayed on board while everyone else put on their scuba gear and headed down to Aquarius.

> **Don wedding attire.** Once aboard Aquarius, the wedding party quickly showered and dressed and proceeded to the ceremony. Although unrehearsed, the ceremony went smoothly. "Before we knew it was over and we were kissing and admiring the shiny new wedding bands on our hands," said Leanne.

> **Make it official.** When they arrived back on shore, their notary public colleague surprised the couple with an intimate champagne celebration to accompany the official notarized signing of the marriage certificate.

When they arrived at their reception, the couple took a few moments together to enjoy the sunset and be photographed by their friends. The atmosphere at the reception was cheerful and relaxed, with plenty of grilled food, cool drinks, and wedding cake. In keeping with tradition, their friends decorated the couple's truck with traditional honeymoon regalia, and the couple departed for several days of relaxation and privacy.

Dealing With the Aftermath of Their Underwater Wedding

"In the beginning, our families were a bit disappointed that they would be unable to attend the underwater ceremony," said Leanne. To accommodate their families' wishes, Leanne and Otto decided to schedule a more traditional ceremony following their honeymoon in Leanne's hometown church. The ceremony was officially a "blessing of the marriage," because they were already legally wed. While the couple was content with their underwater wedding, they recognized that a traditional ceremony would help their loved ones to feel included and would not detract from their original wedding day adventure.

Tips For Other Adventure Wedding Couples

1. **Go for it!** "Although the Aquarius undersea habitat is unavailable for weddings, there are other alternatives," says Leanne. Leanne recommends that couples consider the challenges of the hot sun, afternoon thunderstorms, and mosquitoes if planning an underwater wedding or outdoor reception in the tropics.

2. **Splurge on the traditional accoutrements.** "Arrangements for an underwater photographer and/or videographer may seem extravagant," says Leanne, "but may help those unable to attend the ceremony to understand and

enjoy the experience, especially when displayed at the reception."

3. **Research legal issues.** One final detail that the couple cautions others to watch out for is to be aware that if a Notary Public performs the ceremony, it may not be legally binding if conducted beyond the state's water boundaries.

$ *Leanne and Otto's* $
Underwater Adventure Wedding Details

Honeymoon hotel and travel	= $240
Flowers flowers as reception gifts)	= $0 (Friends gave
Music/Entertainment	= $0 (Couple wanted relaxed, casual reception)
Officiant	= $0 (Colleague volunteered to be Notary Public)
Photography	= $0 (Provided by colleagues and friends)
Bride's dress	= $0 (Borrowed sister's wedding gown)
Groom's attire	= $90 (Rented a tuxedo)
Reception invitations (printed using a computer)	= $50 (Hand-made invitations designed with Aquarius logo)
Reception costs	= $500 (Included cake, homemade appetizers, salads, hamburgers, hotdogs, and liquor) (cont'd)

Wedding rings	= $600
Cake topping	= $60
Marriage License	= $150
Total wedding costs	= $1,690
Total planning time	=3 Months

Underwater Wedding Resources

Many tropical resorts, diving companies, and adventure travel agencies are taking notice of the growing popularity of underwater weddings and offer a variety of underwater wedding packages for couples to choose from. Check out the following resources for more information on planning an underwater wedding:

> **Captain Slate's Atlantis Dive Center**—Also located in Key Largo, this diving center has performed underwater weddings for many years and offers all-inclusive wedding packages. *www.captainslate.com*

> **Four Seasons Resort Maldives**—For an underwater wedding adventure with class, consider the Four Seasons Resort on the Island of Maldives in Kudaa Hura. The island resort, located southwest of Sri Lanka, offers several underwater wedding options. *www.fourseasons.com/maldives*

> **Florida Keys/Key West Chamber of Commerce**—Provides travel and tourism information for this popular destination spot. *www.fla-keys.com*

> **Jules' Undersea Lodge**—Located in Key Largo, this underwater hotel is the only one in the world to offer weddings at five fathoms! Similar to Aquarius in that the hotel also serves as an underwater research laboratory, the lodge's all-inclusive underwater wedding package starts at $1,350. *www.jul.com*

> **Koro Sun Resort**—Located on the enchanted island of Fiji, this resort offers several underwater wedding ceremony packages. *www.korosunresort.com*

> **Maui Ocean Center**—For an underwater wedding in Hawaii for all to experience, consider the Maui Ocean Center, the Hawaiian aquarium. Get married in the aquarium's enormous 750,000-gallon habitat surrounded by family and friends, stingrays and sharks! *www.mauioceancenter.com*

> **National Aquarium of New Zealand**—For a wedding with the sharks, consider getting married at the National Aquarium of New Zealand, which offers underwater wedding packages. *www.nationalaquarium.co.nz*

> **Trang Chamber of Commerce**—The Trang Chamber of Commerce and the Tourism Authority of Thailand have been sponsoring annual underwater wedding festivities since 1996 to promote tourism and adventure. *www.underwaterwedding.com*

Part 3:
Accomplishing a
Non-Traditional
Wedding

Chapter 10

Non-Traditional Wedding Etiquette

The great joy of planning a non-traditional wedding is that you are not held captive by traditional wedding rituals and social mores. You are free to plan the wedding you want without concern for disobeying a wedding custom or offending a wedding guest. Most traditional wedding resources include pages and pages of advice on wedding etiquette, just to make certain that your wedding is the same as everyone else's and that all necessary traditions are attended to. But are there any "rules" that might be helpful to know when planning a non-traditional wedding? The short answer is no, there are no rules that you are bound to follow when planning your non-traditional wedding. The longer answer is that there are some etiquette tips that apply to traditional weddings that can be adapted for your original wedding to make the planning process run more smoothly and successfully. In this chapter, we review 10 of the most significant traditional wedding etiquette tips and modify them so that they are applicable to your unique wedding.

Etiquette Rule #1: Announce Your Engagement

As soon as you become engaged, traditional wedding etiquette commands that you first notify your parents and any children from a previous marriage. The bride's family is told first, and the news should not be a surprise because the groom would have already received marriage permissions from the bride's father. If the groom did not seek prior permission, then the engagement announcement would likely be followed by a questioning period where the bride's parents would express any concerns about the engagement and ultimately provide their blessings. The groom's family is then notified and the mother-of-the-groom contacts the bride's family to express her joy at the engagement. The groom's mother is then expected to encourage the two families to meet and celebrate the approaching wedding.

Many of you are probably reading about this wedding etiquette ritual with dismay. The cool formality and rigidity of the process may be comical to you at best, offensive at worst. The reality is that most non-traditional couples— as well as many traditional ones—do not believe that their wedding plans should be orchestrated by their parents. In many cases, your parents may not even be the first people to hear of your engagement and approaching nuptials. As a non-traditional wedding couple, you and your partner should decide together whom to tell about your wedding plans and when to tell them. Of course, if you are planning a surprise wedding or an elopement, news of your wedding may come much later in the planning process.

As you decide how to announce your engagement or wedding plans to your friends and family, think about the people who are most important to you. Maybe it is really critical for your sister or brother to hear the news first. Maybe you are very close to a best friend and must share the news with her before telling others. Think carefully about whom you want to notify first about your plans and whom you can trust to keep the news private until you have told everyone else. As a unique wedding couple, you have the privilege of being able to share news of your engagement with anyone you want, when you want, without being expected to inform parents before others.

Etiquette Rule #2: Divide Wedding Costs Appropriately

Just as traditional wedding etiquette requires parents to be notified first of wedding day plans, it also expects parents to pay for the wedding celebration. The etiquette rule dictates that the bride's family pay for most of the wedding expenses, with the groom's family hosting the rehearsal dinner and paying for the bride's flowers and the officiant fees. This rule leaves couples with very little power over their wedding day. With moew than 60 percent of today's couples—both traditional and non-traditional—paying for much of their own wedding costs, following this etiquette rule is becoming less popular. Skyrocketing wedding price tags, later-in-life marriages, and couples' increasing desire to have more control of their wedding day lead many brides and grooms to pay for their entire celebration. Approximately 30 percent of today's marrying couples pay for 100 percent of their wedding day costs. Many of these couples are those who choose a non-traditional wedding.

Recognize that when you plan a unique wedding, you should not expect family members to contribute to your wedding fund. It is rather hypocritical to announce to your parents that you have chosen a non-traditional wedding and then demand that they follow tradition by paying for it. That said, many parents will be delighted to hear about your non-traditional nuptials and will be happy to give you a lump sum payment or offer to purchase flowers, pay for a caterer, or buy your wedding announcements. Still, you should be prepared to pay for your entire wedding on your own and not be disappointed if your loved ones do not offer to pay for your wedding. As indicated earlier in this book, money is power, and if you hope to retain control over your wedding day, be very cautious about accepting financial contributions from your loved ones.

Etiquette Rule #3: Select the Wedding Party

According to traditional wedding etiquette, the bride should select her bridesmaids and the groom should select his groomsmen as soon as possible following the engagement. This will allow for the wedding party to help with wedding preparations and provide moral support to the marrying couple. Most traditional weddings that exceed 75 guests generally have at least four bridesmaids and groomsmen, in addition to the maid/matron of honor and the best man. There are certain responsibilities that chosen members of the wedding party are expected to assume in a traditional wedding. The list of obligations can be daunting. Bridesmaids are expected to help the bride select wedding attire; assist with wedding preparations; attend all wedding-related functions, such as showers, luncheons, and rehearsal dinners; throw a bridal shower; and pay for bridesmaid attire. Groomsmen are expected to purchase their own wedding attire, attend all wedding-related functions, host a bachelor party, ensure that all guests have transportation to the reception site, purchase a groom's gift, and assist the bridesmaids. These wedding party responsibilities are extensive and costly and can often contribute to the stress and hassle associated with traditional wedding planning. In fact, bridesmaids have been known to be demoted when they are not able to assist the bride to her satisfaction! Clearly, members of a non-traditional wedding party should not be fettered with the same duties that members of a traditional wedding party would assume. If you are choosing an unconventional wedding that is meant to be relaxed and enjoyable for you and your loved ones, then don't require your bridesmaids and groomsmen to take on traditional functions. For example, don't expect a traditional wedding shower or bachelor party to precede a non-traditional wedding. Your bridesmaids or groomsmen may very well plan a pre-wedding party for you, but you should not expect one.

If you choose to select a wedding party, explain that you are asking people who are important to you to participate in your wedding day. Explain that you do not expect them to take on formal wedding party responsibilities and tell them that you will ask for their help if needed. Many non-traditional wedding couples choose not to include a wedding party at all, or ask a few close loved ones to serve as witnesses to the marriage ceremony. It's your choice who to ask to be closely involved with your wedding; just make sure that if you plan a non-traditional celebration, don't demand that your bridesmaids and groomsmen take on traditional roles.

Etiquette Rule #4: Send Invitations

Traditional wedding invitations are ordered immediately following a couple's engagement and are sent to guests at least two months prior to the wedding date. The wedding stationery is typically white or cream and is printed with black, scripted lettering. Traditional invitations frequently include several components, including the ceremony invitation, a separate reception invitation, a formal reply card, and directions to the ceremony and/or reception site. Traditional wedding etiquette forbids wedding invitations to be sent via e-mail or phone call, and any invitation style that does not conform to the above guidelines is considered tacky. Additionally, traditional wedding etiquette requires handwritten envelopes, not preprinted labels, which are also considered distasteful.

Fortunately for you, your wedding invitations can be as original as you are. You can choose elegant stationery with scripted wording, or you can create your own unique invitation style. Some artistic couples choose to draft their own invitations and have copies made at a local print shop. Other couples choose to purchase themed invitations or to create invitations that include a special poem or passage. Some couples choose to draft a simple, personalized letter to each guest detailing the time and place of the wedding and asking for the guest's attendance. And many couples choose to forgo paper invitations altogether and opt for fun e-mail invitations or personalized phone calls. And all non-traditional couples have the option to produce invitation envelopes with preprinted address labels. How liberating!

There is another traditional wedding etiquette requirement that non-traditional wedding couples may also choose to avoid. Traditional wedding etiquette dictates a separate invitation for the wedding ceremony and wedding reception, although both are usually included in the same envelope. While there is probably a good reason for this, it is difficult to figure out. If you would like to combine your wedding ceremony invitation (or announcement) and the invitation to the post-wedding celebration on the same piece of stationery, then go for it!

Finally, formal wedding etiquette directs wedding guests to properly respond to a wedding invitation by handwriting their response on the reply card. For example, a formal wedding acceptance might read:

Mr. and Mrs. Nelson
accept with pleasure
the invitation of Mr. and Mrs. Riley
to attend their daughter Angela's wedding
to Paul Richardson
On Saturday, the twentieth of June
Two thousand and five
At five o'clock
Trinity Church

If guests decline a wedding invitation, traditional etiquette requires the following response:

Mr. and Mrs. Nelson
regret that they will not be able to accept
the invitation of Mr. and Mrs. Riley
to attend their daughter Angela's wedding
to Paul Richardson
On Saturday, the twentieth of June

Fortunately, non-traditional wedding etiquette is not nearly as rigid—and time-consuming! Many non-traditional couples include an e-mail address for guests to reply to, making it much easier for guests to have a conversation with the lucky couple and encouraging quicker responses and gentle reminders. Unique wedding couples should also be aware that while traditional wedding etiquette usually requires guests who are not able to attend the wedding to send a wedding gift, non-traditional wedding etiquette would not expect such a gesture.

Etiquette Rule #5:
Avoid the Evil Spirits

It has long been considered bad luck for the bride and groom to see each other on their wedding day. In the days of arranged marriages, it was thought that the groom might run away if he saw his bride before the ceremony and she was not appealing to him. This later evolved into a modern day superstition about inviting bad luck if a bride and groom see each other prior to the ceremony. It must be those evil spirits that lurk on one's wedding day! After the rehearsal dinner, most traditional brides and grooms say their farewells and do not see each other until the following day when the bride walks down the aisle toward her groom.

Many non-traditional couples choose to ignore wedding superstitions and related etiquette rules. For example, the non-traditional couples featured in this book talk about sharing special moments together prior to their wedding ceremony, such as going for a morning jog or enjoying a quiet lunch. You are likely choosing a non-traditional wedding because you value being together as a couple on your wedding day. So spend time with each other before your ceremony, and don't worry about those evil spirits!

Etiquette Rule #6: Exchange Traditional Vows

Traditional weddings feature an exchange of vows, typically before a religious official. Many couples who choose to marry in a place of worship, such as a synagogue, mosque, or church, must attend pre-marital counseling classes to make certain that the couple is prepared to unite with the church and raise their family according to the church's religious beliefs. This preparation is then reflected in a traditional ceremony and standard exchange of vows. While "love, honor, and obey" and other such hegemonic phrases have been abandoned from many traditional ceremonies, the weighty tone of a traditional wedding ceremony remains.

Many non-traditional wedding couples want their wedding day to be more free and uplifting. They want a ceremony

and vows that reflect their individuality and caring relationship. If you want to create a wedding ceremony and
vows that are personal to you, you have many options. Many
books that are currently on the market focus exclusively
on creating personalized ceremonies and preparing meaningful vows. Additionally, many Websites have emerged to
offer ceremony suggestions and sample vows.

Ironically, to find some non-traditional ceremony and
vow ideas, you may turn to traditional resources. A great
place to start searching for vow ideas is to visit the Websites
of churches in your neighborhood. Many churches have a
variety of vows that couples can choose from, and these
suggestions can give you a starting place to draft your own
exchanges. For my elopement, for example, I visited a
church Website and tailored its suggested online vows to
our individual wishes. This is what we came up with for our
non-traditional vows:

> "Brian, I take you as my husband. I pledge to
> share my life openly with you, to speak the truth to
> you in love. I promise to honor and tenderly care for
> you, to cherish and encourage your own fulfillment
> as an individual through all the changes of our lives."

For the exchange of rings ceremony, we said the following:

> "Brian, take this ring as a symbol of my love
> and promise, and with all that I am and all that I
> have, with this ring I thee wed, now and forever."

You have as much freedom as you would like when
creating your non-traditional wedding ceremony and exchanging your personal wedding vows. Be sure to let your
officiant, or wedding coordinator, know ahead of time if
you will be incorporating your own vows into the ceremony.
Also, you may want to ask the officiant to send you a sample
of his wedding ceremony script so that you can make sure
that it is appropriate for your wedding. While you want to

find the right officiant for your ceremony, try not to be unreasonable. For example, if your officiant wants to allude to God or other religious symbols in her ceremony and you would prefer for these references to be kept to a minimum, share your concerns with the officiant but also be respectful of her religious beliefs. If you and your officiant cannot compromise effectively, find another officiant or justice of the peace who will collaborate with you to create a unique ceremony and accept unconventional vows.

To truly personalize your ceremony and involve your loved ones, you may also want to think about asking a family member or friend to serve as your officiant. Many states allow laypeople to become a notary public or wedding celebrant without much hassle. Check with your Secretary of State's office or town clerk to learn about wedding officiant requirements in your area.

Resources for Preparing Your Wedding Vows

Check out these helpful resources for writing your own vows, modifying traditional sayings, or exploring new ways to say I do with a twist:

Complete Book of Wedding Vows by Diane Warner (Career Press, 1996). A tremendous resource for couples seeking help on how to write their own vows or meaningfully incorporate traditional vows into a personalized ceremony.

With These Words...I Thee Wed: Contemporary Wedding Vows for Today's Couples by Barbara Eklof (Adams Media, 1989). Written by a wedding consultant with experience planning non-traditional weddings, this book offers resources to help you convey your true emotions on your wedding day.

Wedding Vows: Beyond Love, Honor and Cherish by Susan Lee Smith (Warner Books, 2001). This book provides helpful hints on how to create a contemporary wedding ceremony.

The Everything Wedding Vows Book: Anything and Everything You Could Possibly Say at the Altar - And Then Some by Janet Anastasio, et al. (Adams Media, 2001). This book offers dozens of techniques for developing personalized wedding vows for any type of wedding service.

Etiquette Rule #7: Have Your Cake

Traditional weddings often feature an elaborate wedding cake featured prominently at the reception site for all to gawk at. It is also often accompanied by a smaller, darker groom's cake. Due to the large size and expense of today's traditional weddings, many featured weddings cakes are for decoration only. The guests are encouraged to look, but not eat! After the cake-cutting ceremony, guests are often given slices of another sheet cake prepared in the kitchen to avoid ruining the decorative cake. Traditional wedding etiquette and superstition also request that couples save the top tier of their decorative wedding cake in their freezer for one year and then eat a slice on their first anniversary to ensure good luck.

Non-traditional wedding couples are typically more practical in their wedding planning and often choose function over frills. While many unique wedding couples still choose to cut a cake on their wedding day, they often avoid the formalities and expense associated with decorative cakes in favor of simpler cakes or creative desserts. They also often take their chances with the evil spirits and avoid freezing their cake!

In your non-traditional wedding and celebration, you have the privilege of choosing a cake or dessert selection that is appropriate for you, and not one that is required for wedding pageantry.

Etiquette Rule #8: Give a Wedding Toast

Traditional wedding receptions include a toast by the best man and any others who wish to acknowledge the couple's marriage. The wedding couple is typically silent during the wedding reception, thanking guests privately during the receiving line and individually throughout the reception.

Post-wedding celebrations for non-traditional weddings are often more personalized. It is a nice gesture for couples to make an announcement thanking their guests for attending their wedding ceremony or post-wedding celebration. If the guests who attend your post-wedding celebration did not attend your wedding, as in the case of an elopement, destination wedding, or adventure wedding, you might want to consider explaining that while you chose to celebrate your *wedding* privately, you want to share your *marriage* with those you love and care about for many years to come. Personal acknowledgements from the bride and groom to their guests can add a level of class to your non-traditional celebration and express to your loved ones your reasons for choosing something different for your wedding day. These acknowledgements also reinforce that you chose a unique wedding because it was right for you, and not to hurt or disappoint your friends and family.

Etiquette Rule #9:
Embark on Your Honeymoon

For most traditional couples, a wedding is quickly followed by a honeymoon, which, according to traditional etiquette, is paid for by the groom and his family. For non-traditional couples, a honeymoon is often incorporated into a wedding celebration or postponed until a later date. Elopers, destination wedding couples, and wedding adventurers often combine their wedding celebration and honeymoon to enjoy several days of fun and relaxation and to reduce wedding expenses. For some non-traditional couples, a honeymoon is often a large expense that is not paid for by the groom's family, but by the couple. These couples frequently choose to wait several months or a year before taking a trip to celebrate their wedding. And some non-traditional wedding couples choose to forgo a honeymoon altogether. Perhaps the derivation of the honeymoon as a time when a man captured his bride and kept her intoxicated for several days is a turn-off for some think-different couples!

Etiquette Rule #10: Send Thank You Notes

Here, tradition and its opposite meet. Regardless of what type of wedding you plan, you should always say thank you to your guests for their wedding gifts and support. But as with much of your non-traditional wedding planning, your thank you notes can—and should—be personalized and unique and written by both the bride and the groom. You can purchase standard thank you notes at a stationery store, have thank you notes printed on creative or themed card stock, or design your own thank you cards. Either way, each of your thank you notes should be personally tailored to the receiver. Talk about the significance of the gift, the generosity of the sender, and how you will use the gift in your new life. While most non-traditional wedding etiquette allows for e-mail communications, you should try to send handwritten thank you notes to express your fullest gratitude.

Traditional wedding etiquette allows busy brides to send gift acknowledgement cards if they are not able to send formal thank you notes within three months of the wedding. These impersonal acknowledgement cards often read as follows:

Mrs. Paul Richardson

wishes to acknowledge the receipt

of your wedding gift

and will contact you later of her appreciation

Non-traditional wedding couples should desperately avoid this traditional ritual. For any wedding, traditional or not, preprinted acknowledgement cards send a message of cool indifference. For non-traditional couples especially, they may also promote the stereotypes you are trying to avoid. They may indicate that you are too self-absorbed to care about others and make it appear that you want to continue to distance yourself from your family and friends.

Send simple, personalized, handwritten thank you notes no more than one month after you receive wedding gifts to express your sincere gratitude and to remind your loved ones that you care deeply about their support.

It's liberating to think that you do not need to be bound by the same etiquette rules that traditional brides and grooms must obey. You have the luxury of setting your own rules and customizing a wedding celebration that is free from obligation. Just remember that when you select a non-traditional wedding, you should not expect your loved ones to assume traditional roles and responsibilities. While it is often more challenging to create new traditions than to follow those that have been with us for centuries, the rewards you will gain by creating your own rules will be far worth the effort.

One of the greatest challenges for non-traditional couples is how to deal with the aftermath of a non-traditional wedding and the varied reactions of family members and friends. A topic not found in any traditional wedding etiquette book, the etiquette of dealing with the aftermath of your unique wedding is deserving of an entire chapter in this guide.

Chapter 11

Congratulations? Not Always

Dealing With the Aftermath of Your Non-Traditional Wedding

Cairo, Egypt—Nora Marzouk Ahmed was on her honeymoon Tuesday when her father chopped off her head and carried it down a dusty neighborhood street as a punishment for dishonoring the family. Her crime: She had eloped.[1]

News of your non-traditional wedding will likely not cause your loved ones the same despair that poor Nora's father experienced. But it is very likely that you will encounter some disapproval from friends and family to your non-traditional wedding. Many couples who choose a non-traditional wedding report that a negative reaction from loved ones is one of the most startling and distressing aspects of their wedding. Nearly all of the non-traditional wedding couples featured in this book describe mixed responses to their wedding selection. This chapter will help you to brace yourself for negative reactions and learn how to cultivate positive responses so that you can deal with the aftermath of your non-traditional wedding and avoid getting your head chopped off!

You have participated in enjoyable, stress-free wedding planning; reveled in making wedding decisions alongside your partner; designed a perfect wedding day for you and your spouse; and are looking forward to beginning a new life as husband and wife. Now you declare your marriage intentions (or your new marital status), to the world and let the chips fall where they may.

You will find that most of your loved ones greet your marriage with exaltation! Your married friends will share with you the unspoken truth that their traditional wedding day wasn't all it was cracked up to be, that the party was over before it started, that if they had it to do over again they would have loved to do something original and exciting. If your wedding plans involve minimal costs, you will probably encounter many people who tell you that they wish they had used their wedding money for something more long-lasting than a four-hour reception. After all, how many people do you know who, at the end of their wedding reception, say, "Gosh, I am so glad that I just spent 20 thousand dollars on that party!"? Far more likely, you will hear the truth that the fanfare of a traditional wedding is overrated and overpriced.

You will also hear the sincere admiration from many friends and family who praise your unique wedding and comment on the creativity and romance of your idea. You may have friends and family members in the process of their own wedding-planning who take a step back and reevaluate why it is they are planning the large, traditional wedding. Overall, you should hear in most people's voices and see in most people's eyes heartfelt joy and excitement at the news of your wedding. But you might as well be warned now that there may be those few acquaintances who will react to your unique wedding with unexpected hostility. You must also prepare yourself that some of these disgruntled acquaintances may very well be your dearest friends and closest family members.

Hopefully, news of your non-traditional wedding will bring nothing but joy and happiness to those around you. But as you decide if a non-traditional wedding is right for you, you should make certain that you are prepared to face the criticism and disappointment of your loved ones. If the thought of your best friend, favorite aunt, or beloved grandfather condemning your different wedding outweighs the many reasons why you decided to have a unique wedding, then you may need to reconsider your wedding options. If you think you are strong enough and committed enough to walking down the aisle of your own choosing, then prepare yourself for the inevitable.

Non-traditional wedding couples share interesting stories about the aftermath of their unique wedding. While acknowledging that they expected some resistance and disappointment, many were surprised that the people whom they expected to react negatively were among their staunchest supporters, while those they anticipated would be happy by the news reacted with tears and sadness. One eloper's grandmother simply scowled at every detail of her wedding, looked at photographs of the day begrudgingly, and proceeded to talk about all of the wonderful (traditional) weddings that she had been to or was planning to attend.

Other alternative wedding couples expressed their shock at the selfish reactions of friends and family. One bride who chose a small adventure wedding told of the reaction of a favorite uncle who exploded in anger at being deprived of the right to see his niece walk down the aisle and participate in her wedding day. A destination wedding couple shared the startling response of a very religious and traditional older aunt who, upon hearing the news of their wedding, proclaimed: "Oh, how horrible! Well that marriage won't last." And, of course, it wouldn't be the first time that a loved one proclaims that your non-traditional wedding plans are a result of the fact that you are pregnant.

Hopefully you will not be met with such extreme examples of disappointment, selfishness, and condemnation, but it is important that you prepare yourself for the possibility. While you may not experience such blatant reactions, you are likely to be disappointed by the reactions of some friends and family members who are less than excited by your news. Some friends may react coolly to the news of your unique wedding, with forced congratulations and well-wishes. Other friends and acquaintances may simply not know how they should react to your unconventional wedding and may change the subject or approach the news with odd indifference. Friends and colleagues, who may have spent hundreds of dollars on wedding gifts, celebratory dinners, wedding showers, golf outings, and bachelor/bachelorette parties for other to-be-married or recently married friends, may do nothing to celebrate your wedding. A bride planning a destination wedding with her parents to Italy, for instance, was shocked by the response she received after e-mailing four of her close friends with news of her unique wedding. She received one response of congratulations, one apathetic response, and no responses at all from the remaining two friends.

The mixed reactions to a non-traditional wedding highlight the disappointing fact that most traditional wedding celebrations are robotic rituals. When you throw a different kind of wedding into the mix, friends often don't know how to react. Because of this phenomenon, you can take comfort in knowing that the friends who celebrate with you are genuinely happy about your marriage and are not simply keeping score. Reactions to your non-traditional wedding can tell you a lot about your friends and family. True friends will be truly happy. Less than true friends will not.

How to React to Negative Feedback

If you have made it this far along in the book, clearly you are considering a non-traditional wedding because it is meaningful to you. You recognize that your wedding day is about you and your partner, and not about several hundred guests packed into a sterile function hall. You acknowledge that although you look forward to sharing the rest of your married life surrounded by close friends and family, your wedding day celebrates the commitment you and your partner make to one another. Therefore, while it is important for you to prepare yourself for surprising scowls and snares, it is equally important that you reaffirm that your wedding day is *your* wedding day.

So how should you react to those disappointing, often maddening, responses? First of all, be strong. The negative comments of friends and family are an attempt to castigate you for being defiant and escaping tradition. The negative people want you to regret your wedding decision as much as they do. They want you to apologize for hurting them and admit that, indeed, you were wrong to choose a nontraditional wedding. Don't let them succeed! While it is much easier said than done, it is important that you not let these negative people lessen your commitment to a unique wedding day or hijack your beautiful wedding memories. Explain firmly, but pleasantly, how happy you are with your wedding decision and explain what a very special day it will be—or was—for you and your partner. Avoid criticizing traditional weddings when explaining your reasons for wanting an alternative wedding, as this makes it appear that you doubt your own judgment. Simply state the truth: that while a traditional wedding is the right choice for many people, it was not right for you.

If the negative person continues to be negative, you may need to say something a bit more assertive, such as, "I can see that you are not happy or supportive of our wedding decision. My wedding day will be (or was), filled with happiness and joy and I ask that if you cannot be happy along with us, then please keep your negative comments to yourself." If the person's criticisms persist, simply walk away. You should not feel the need to apologize because of the objectionable reactions of a few selfish loved ones. You do not need to justify your actions to anyone. If anything, negative reactions to your wedding should give you relief. After all, if these people react this poorly to your non-traditional wedding plans, just imagine the battles that would have been fought while planning a traditional wedding!

And how do you react to the whispers and glares from family and friends who wonder when you will be announcing your pregnancy? The stereotypical images of non-traditional weddings and elopements remain engrained in the minds of many of your loved ones, and so it should not surprise you that many people will assume you chose an unusual wedding to avoid an out-of-wedlock pregnancy. Many couples remark that this response is the most distressing because their loved ones do not truly understand the purpose and meaning of their unique wedding. If you are confronted with skeptical loved ones, simply take comfort in knowing that when you don't give birth in nine months, they will know that you aren't pregnant!

After you have done your best to ignore negative comments and allow criticisms to roll off your back, try to cut some slack to those loved ones who may be less than supportive of your wedding decision. Indeed, they have been brainwashed by the same Traditional Wedding Monopoly that you confronted and it may take them awhile to accept and appreciate an alternative wedding day paradigm. Avoid discussing your wedding with these disinterested people, as it will only lead to consternation and conjure resentment. Resume your relationship where it was before you revealed the news of your unique wedding plans. While it may take some time for you to get over the surprising reactions to your wedding, it is probably not worth severing relationships with friends and family simply because they do not understand why you chose something out of the ordinary for your wedding. Remember that you and your partner are the only ones who really need to know why an unconventional wedding is the perfect wedding option for you.

As you consider the aftermath of your original wedding, you should also prepare yourself for a phenomenon unique to non-traditional wedding announcements: The Delayed Reaction. Many couples report that when they initially announced their non-traditional wedding plans to loved ones, they were pleasantly surprised by the immediate response. Hugs of joy and cries of happiness allowed them to breathe a sigh of relief at the moment they were most dreading over the previous weeks. Whew! That wasn't so bad after all, they thought. The trouble generally begins a few days after the wedding announcement as the reality of the event begins to sink in. Mothers and mothers-in-law, grandmothers, aunts, sisters, and best friends begin to realize that you have excluded them from a traditional wedding day extravaganza. Often, the initial excitement from family and friends of your unique wedding is replaced later with feelings of disappointment, hurt, and rejection. Loved ones may try to convince you to have a traditional wedding and reception or make you feel guilty for choosing something different. It is important to prepare yourself for these delayed responses and to remind your loved ones that you did not choose a non-traditional wedding in an effort to hurt them. You chose a different kind of wedding because it was right for you.

"I was 18 when I met my husband who was 19 and from a very backwoods community in Kentucky. We decided to elope because my parents were dead set against the idea of us marrying so young. My father worked with a couple of men whose daughters had married young, had babies, and were left by their husbands when times got too tough. He was afraid the same would happen to me.

"We decided to elope on Labor Day weekend (September 5, 1964) when we knew everyone would be down on Cape Cod at my parents' cottage. I thought we would go back to our lives and hide the fact we were married for a little while, but my husband had other plans. He got right on the phone to the Cape and when my father answered the phone my husband said, "Howdy, this is your new son-in-law." My father was furious and told us to get down to the Cape right away. When we arrived the first question of course was 'Oh my god, are you pregnant?' I was not.

"My sisters were angry because they felt cheated out of being bridesmaids.

"I hate to be the center of attention, so I have no regrets. I think if I had to plan a big wedding, it might not have happened. My parents, it turns out, found my husband to be a blessing. My brother was killed a few years later and my husband ended up becoming like a second son to them. They gave their blessing to my two other sisters when they got married, and my parents don't have nearly as wonderful a relationship with those sons-in-law.

"The thing that made me most angry was that a girl I worked with got married around the same time—big wedding, white dress, the whole shebang. We both announced that we were pregnant around the same time. Because I eloped everyone started counting back the months from my delivery, but when the other woman gave birth two months before me, everyone was only surprised that her preemie was so big!"

How to React to Positive Feedback

Reacting to negative feedback regarding your unique wedding may very well be your biggest wedding challenge. The good news is that most couples say they encountered only a few negative responses and focused on surrounding themselves with the people who were delighted with their original wedding idea. When you encounter these support-ive people, be sure to let them know how much their loy-alty means to you. While traditional wedding etiquette allows for a three-month turnaround on thank you notes, your wedding thank-yous should be sent much, much sooner. Brief, heartfelt, personalized thank you notes should be sent no later than *one month* after you receive a wedding gift. Why so soon? Because this way you continue to acknowledge that one of the primary reasons you decided to have a non-traditional wedding was not to shun family and friends, but the opposite: to make your wedding a more meaningful, less me-chanical, experience. Responding quickly to your loved ones' generosity and thoughtfulness also reinforces your heartfelt gratitude for their well-wishes and demonstrates that you are eager to include them in your long-lasting, happy marriage.

$ Wedding Planning Price Tag $
Thank You Notes (50 count)

Traditional thank you note stationery and envelopes printed by a specialty store vendor	Estimated Cost: $150
Traditional (blank) thank you note stationery and envelopes purchased at a stationery store	Estimated Cost: $50
Printed thank you notes and envelopes purchased online	Estimated Cost: $75

Coping with the reactions of friends and family to your unconventional wedding may be a difficult wedding obstacle for you. Fortunately, you will discover that most of your loved ones are overjoyed at the individuality and originality of your wedding day. They will shower you with blessings and support, and you will in turn shower them with gratitude and devotion. But you will also likely encounter loved ones who are not pleased about your wedding and you will need to react with patience and understanding to their rebukes. Your best defense in dealing with these challenges is to anticipate them before your wedding day. Acknowledging ahead of time that there may be some disappointment with your unique wedding will enable you to defend yourself against getting your head chopped off by disapproving friends and family!

Chapter Note

1. Tarek El-Tablawy, "Woman Decapitated for Eloping: Dad Acts to Restore Family's Honor." *Peoria Journal Star*, 20 August 1997.

Chapter 12

Post-Wedding Celebration Ideas

Many couples choose to deal with the aftermath of their non-traditional wedding by planning a post-wedding celebration following their unique ceremony. Many choose a small wedding ceremony and want to celebrate later with their larger group of friends and family members. Some opt for a private, personal ceremony but want a grand wedding celebration. And many non-traditional couples decide to plan a post-wedding celebration to satisfy the wishes of loved ones. If you decide to plan a post-wedding celebration, there are many party ideas to choose from. You could consider a theme celebration or a surprise party, like those discussed earlier in this book, or you could plan another type of gala. This chapter offers post-wedding celebration suggestions that help you to prolong your wedding extravaganza while limiting your stress and worry.

Why Plan a Post-Wedding Celebration?

Some of you may be wondering why you would bother to plan a post-wedding party. Isn't the purpose of your non-traditional wedding to avoid the pomp and circumstance associated with traditional wedding fanfare? Many couples who plan a non-traditional wedding are surprised to learn just how much a celebration in honor of their marriage means to those closest to them. "I was struck by how important it was to my family and friends to be included in a wedding celebration," said Amanda Trombley after planning her murder mystery theme wedding party. "I wanted to do something for them." And many couples also want to plan something to commemorate their marriage and enjoy time with loved ones. The primary difference between traditional wedding receptions and the post-wedding celebrations that so many non-traditional wedding couples plan is that the latter are much more relaxed, uncomplicated, guest-oriented affairs. While it is true that post-wedding celebrations can easily explode into full-fledged traditional wedding receptions, they can escape this fate with some careful planning. As you begin to think about the type of post-wedding celebration you will plan, here are some questions to consider:

What Is the Primary Reason for Your Celebration?

You and your partner should discuss why you want to plan a post-wedding celebration. Is it to get together with friends and family? Is it to appease your parents or loved ones? Is it to add some formality and tradition to a unique wedding celebration? Deciding on the purpose of your post-wedding celebration will help to make the planning go more smoothly. If you are like many couples who give in to a post-wedding celebration because parents are desperate to throw you a wedding reception, then you may decide to turn over all control to these party planners and let them create their dream reception without being involved in the planning's chaos.

If you want to plan your own celebration, or at least have more control over a party that others host for you, then consider what is most important to you and set some parameters. If you don't want the party to look like a traditional wedding reception, then make your wishes known and explain that you will be hosting an enjoyable party, not a typical wedding gala. Getting your cohosts to start thinking of your celebration as a *party* and not a wedding reception is likely to ease tensions and make preparations more relaxed.

You also may want to set parameters around traditions associated with a wedding celebration. Guests may expect to dress in a certain way, shower you with gifts, and witness traditional wedding reception activities, such as first dances, toasts, sit-down meals, and cake-cutting ceremonies. If you don't want guests to behave in traditional wedding reception fashion, then let them know ahead of time what to expect at your post-wedding celebration. You may include wording on your party invitation that alludes to a "casual celebration to commemorate our recent marriage," or a "Sunday brunch with friends and family." If you don't want your guests to feel obligated to purchase wedding gifts for you, tell them individually or on your invitation that their "presence not presents" is what is most important to you. Many non-traditional wedding couples—and an increasing number of traditional couples—request that guests donate money to the couple's favorite charity in lieu of wedding gifts.

As you begin to plan your post-wedding celebration, realize that you are in control of your party just as you were your wedding. Set expectations and ground rules. Anticipate guest concerns and questions. Be creative and don't feel bound to traditional wedding reception rituals.

When Do You Want to Host Your Post-Wedding Celebration?

Some non-traditional wedding couples, particularly those who plan elopements and destination weddings, are eager to host a post-wedding party soon after they return from a wedding-away. While they enjoyed the peacefulness and privacy of an intimate wedding, they are eager to soon be surrounded by their friends and loved ones. Other couples may decide to plan their post-wedding celebration months after their wedding. This is especially true for couples who may need to travel to several cities to celebrate with friends and family members scattered around the globe. Think about how much time you will need to plan your party and how much notice you would like to give to your guests. To keep your post-wedding celebration a relaxed affair, consider planning your party around a holiday such as the Fourth of July, Labor Day, Thanksgiving, New Year's Eve, or St. Patrick's Day. People often prefer to get together at these times and will enjoy celebrating two special occasions. Some couples also decide to plan their post-wedding celebration on their first anniversary to commemorate this milestone.

You may want to weave some of your wedding day memories into your post-wedding celebration. If you got married on a tropical island, consider a luau-themed party. If you got married in Italy, cook up a grand Italian dinner for your guests. If you got married underwater, plan a pool party. Incorporating elements of your wedding day into your post-wedding celebration can make your guests feel more connected to your unique wedding and can illustrate to them the originality of your day. Consider passing around your wedding photos or creating a photo collage of your wedding day. Schedule some time for your guests to view your wedding day video. Wear your wedding day attire. Restate your vows in front of your guests. These party touches can add special meaning to your celebration and involve your guests. Try hard, however, not to overload your partygoers with your wedding paraphernalia. Encourage them to have a great time in your honor!

What Type of Post-Wedding Celebration Do You Want?

Just as you undertook a deliberate process to select the type of non-traditional wedding that was right for you, so too you will want to plan a post-wedding celebration that suits you best. Maybe you planned an informal wedding ceremony and would like a more formal post-wedding celebration. If so, start looking into function hall rates and availability, or consider having your celebration catered at your home or a friend's home. Begin shopping for your party essentials such as entertainment, decorations, flowers, food, and favors. If you would like a more informal, or less traditional party, think about a breakfast or brunch party, a Sunday afternoon fall football party, a Friday night cocktail party, or a backyard cookout. Whichever party style you choose, formal or informal, remember to be wary of telling vendors that your party is related to a wedding. Costs will climb and rigid pricing plans may limit your ability to customize your own unique post-wedding celebration.

Post-Wedding Celebration Ideas

> Rent out a room or section at your favorite restaurant to celebrate with close family and friends.

> Host a Sunday brunch party at a local hotel, restaurant, or private residence.

> Use the Theme Weddings chapter (Chapter 8) to plan a post-wedding theme party.

> Plan your celebration to coincide with your first anniversary.

> Tie your post-wedding celebration to a lively holiday, milestone birthday, or sporting event.

> For guests traveling far-and-wide, find a large rental property and plan a multi-day post-wedding celebration.

> Plan an elegant cocktail party on a Thursday evening when function hall rates are greatly reduced, calendars are free, and guests are eager to ring in the weekend.

> For golf fanatics, plan a golf tournament celebration, or for ski bums, plan a fun family trip to the mountains.

> Host a family reunion to gather loved ones together.

> Plan a vow renewal ceremony and reception to involve guests unable to attend your unique wedding.

> Allow an eager friend or family member to plan your celebration for you.

> Plan a formal, traditional wedding reception.

Post-Wedding Celebration Planning Timeline

Now that you have thought about why you want a post-wedding celebration, when you want it, and what type of party it will be, let the planning begin! As most non-traditional couples agree, planning a post-wedding celebration can often be far more time-consuming and stressful than your unique wedding. Use these party planning steps to get started with your preparations:

At Least 6 Weeks Prior

> Decide on a party budget.

> Finalize your guest list.

> Select party date, time, and style.

> Select and reserve a party location.

> Contact party vendors, such as caterers, entertainers, and tent rental companies. If you will be hosting the party yourself, decide what type of food and party activities you would like to include.

> Purchase or order party invitations.

2 to 4 Weeks Prior

> Mail/e-mail invitations at least three weeks prior to the party. Don't forget to include a desired R.S.V.P. date!

> Inform guests about party expectations, including proper attire and format. Let them know your expectations about gifts. If you have registered for gifts, casually let guests know where to shop for you.

> Finalize your party menu.

> Visit party supply stores and discount wholesale stores to select party decorations and party favors.

> Purchase disposable cameras for candid shots of your guests.

> If many children will be present at your party, consider hiring a babysitter to relieve parents.

1 Week Prior

> Call any guests that have not yet responded to your invitation.

> Plan your party's agenda, including time for toasts, activities, and entertainment.

> Visit the party location prior to your celebration to confirm contractual agreements, locate restrooms and coatrooms to direct your guests, and coordinate decorations.

> Make certain that there will be both alcoholic and non-alcoholic beverages available for your guests.

1 to 3 Days Prior

> Shop for any last-minute party details, such as groceries, clothing accessories, and decorations.

> Confirm with vendors.

> Purchase and prepare your thank you notes to send immediately following your party to thank your guests for attending—even if they don't bring gifts.

> Get decorations ready.

> Have a great time!

A post-wedding party is a wonderful way to bring family members and friends together to celebrate your recent nuptials. Your loved ones will enjoy feeling connected to your wedding and you will be able to reinforce to them that they are an important part of your life even if you did not choose a traditional wedding. You have many party options to choose from. Decide what type of party you want and who you want to be in control of the planning. If you will be involved in the preparations, be clear about your party parameters and expectations and select a party style that feels right to you. Follow some simple party planning steps to make the process run smoothly and, as always, beware of the term "wedding" when interacting with party vendors!

Epilogue

While writing this book, I was struck by how many non-traditional wedding couples said they would have loved to have a resource devoted to helping them plan their unique wedding. Many had to rely on traditional wedding books and magazines that offered one-size-fits-all wedding ideas and planning steps. Several said they had no idea how many other couples choose to plan unique weddings and were pleased to know that they are among a large and growing group of think-different couples.

After reading this book, hopefully you feel inspired by the stories of other non-traditional brides and grooms who have pioneered new wedding visions, and you now have the tools you need to plan your tailor-made wedding. You may have gravitated to one of the five suggested unique wedding options, or used these recommendations to explore another non-traditional wedding adventure. Or maybe after reading this book and considering many traditional wedding alternatives, you feel that a traditional wedding is really what you want. The purpose of this book was to provide choices: to show you that you are not *required* to plan a certain type of wedding, but are free to explore many creative wedding options and select the one that feels right.

Planning your wedding is an exciting and fun life event. Whichever wedding option you ultimately choose, you should feel good about your decision and eager to celebrate this special occasion. May you enjoy many years of marital bliss after you say I do with a twist!

For more non-traditional wedding resources and support, or to post your own non-traditional wedding planning success story, please visit this book's Website at: *www.weddingtwist.com.*

Index